A wo
where
everyone
plays

Finding a way to bring fun and excitement back into learning

EDITED BY

Bernadette E. Ashby

EFTING

E

PRESS

Sunnyvale, California

A World Where Everyone Plays
Copyright © 2010 by Bernadette E. Ashby

FIRST EDITION, 2011

Printed in the United States of America

Book Design by Tim Dere
Photography Courtesy of Kristin M. Young Photography

ISBN 978-1-60330-001-8

Published by Efting Press
SAN 853-3040

To order additional copies of **A World Where Everyone Plays** or to contact the editor go to www.fortheluvofpiano.com.
To contact Simply Music go to www.simplymusic.com.

Dedicated to...

...the person who has always wanted to play

...and to my musical children,
Victoria, Abigayle, and Hunter.

§§§

In Loving Memory of Coach John Scolinos,

March 28, 1918 – November 7, 2009,

my hero and the inspiration behind my teaching.

ACKNOWLEDGEMENTS

Breakthroughs are common in Simply Music. This book is no different. I never imagined myself editing or co-authoring a book of this caliber, working with the best – talented, most astute, sensitive colleagues. I owe it all to the undying support of my family, friends, and the Simply Music community. It's been a privilege – one of the wildest adventures that I have ever taken. My loving thanks goes to...

...my husband, Myron, for believing more in the dream than I did. I couldn't have done it without your faithful love and support.

...my children, Victoria, Abigayle, and Hunter, for sacrificing the time that you could have spent with Mom. I love you with an everlasting love.

...the Simply Music teachers, parents, and staff for generously providing the stories to make this book possible. What an amazing community that you are! I'm proud to be a part of this family.

...Dr. Linda Maram, for your academic inspiration and assisting with the editing.

...Jeanette Lavoie, for your unceasing prayers and authoring insights.

...The Adams, Burkes, Kirouacs, Kelleys, and Allens, for willingly watching my kids when I needed you.

...Cathy Hirata, for lending me your ear and being my 'partner in crime'.

...my studio parents and students. I couldn't ask for a more fantastic and cooperative bunch to work with. Thank you for the privilege of teaching you and your children.

...Phillip Maroc, for your legal advice.

...Tim Dere, for your amazing cover design, formatting assistance, and knowledgeable marketing insights. Thanks for contributing to this miracle of a book and for being a great friend over the years.

...Kristin M. Young, for being the most artistic photographer that I know and one of the most supportive parents ever.

...Gail Efting, for the hundreds of hours that you spent with me to help me birth this dream of a book. Your investment is eternal. You are a Godsend.

...Neil Moore. Without you, there is no Simply Music. Thank you for giving me and tens of thousands of others the gift of music.

Ultimately, in the fashion of J. S. Bach, Soli Deo Gloria.

TABLE OF CONTENTS

FOREWORD

A World Where Everyone Plays. What would that look like? What does that mean? How would it change us? "World" and "everyone" is all encompassing – all human beings. "Plays" insinuates action. Am I saying that every single human being should become piano players? Play a musical instrument? That would be an ideal world, but, alas, we don't live in a perfect world. But there is a way...

When they find out that I'm a piano teacher, most adults say, "Oh, I took piano lessons as a kid...but I hated doing scales... It was boring...It wasn't fun." Occasionally, I'll run into a person that still plays mostly as a hobby. By my estimates, one out of ten people I meet continue playing the piano from childhood. This average tells a "story". The irony of it all is that many parents who have taken lessons as a child, despite their failures, insist that their children take lessons. Why? Because they understand the intrinsic value that music can bring into their very lives – how it can form character, increase intellect, and lay a foundation for so many skills. Unfortunately, the "story" that is being told is that piano lessons are not working. Too many students become piano dropouts.

Perhaps, a new approach is needed, one that could 'rock' the piano world. A method that is so simple that it's confounding the current system. An approach that is so much fun that it is attracting thousands of students around the world. A system that is so powerful that it not only can teach you how to play the piano *easily*, but also change a life; reaching for impossibilities, creating breakthroughs, and making dreams come true.

Music is such a wonderful conduit for so many things. Taking lessons teaches us the value of discipline, perseverance, and excellence. Music can touch our souls in ways nothing else can. And through music we can enter into another world; a world of creativity, passion, exploration, discovery, and joy in learning. Through music as an art form, we can truly express what's inside of us – contribute to the world in such a way that we can affect change – a fulfillment of the fundamental need to express ourselves. So the real question at hand may not be "should everyone play?" but, "What would the world look like if we truly expressed ourselves in our own unique way, that which we were meant to do and be?" Our world would be different.

The world needs more individuals that are self-expressed. Self-expressed people are a creative people, dynamic in culture. They are critical-thinkers, problem-solvers, trouble-shooters, contributors to the greater good. Self-expression creates generations of inventors, designers, entrepreneurs, consultants, engineers, leaders, analysts, pioneers in their field, etc. A self-expressed culture applies creative solutions to *any* problem. Our jobs and tasks are seen as a love rather than an obligation because we are working within the realm of that which we were created for.

Self-expression is an inherent need for all human beings. It gives us purpose because we are living within our calling. It gives us joy because we are fulfilled. Without it, life can feel meaningless, empty – like the office worker who goes through life day in and day out, or the mom who longs for more than picking up after her family, or the student who is completely absorbed in the rigors of academia, or the CEO who is tired of the rat race. Life is habitual, automatic; it takes its daily course for years. Where in life does a person like this have an opportunity to invent, create, or design? Where are they allowed to pursue and express their passions so they can make the world a better place?

In a consumer culture, music is not owned by us; music is done to us. The onset of technology has contributed to this. When the radio entered the world, all of a sudden, we could take music anywhere with us – in the kitchen, in our automobiles, at work. However, it also limited our musical activity because it initiated the move away from making music. The plethora of ipods, mp3s, and musical mediums proves this.

On the contrary, the ability to produce empowers us, encourages us, and gives us life. By giving people a venue to become self-expressed, it just may be the spark to awaken them to the potential within. And that spark cannot help but grow and translate into other areas because of the confidence it gives. It cannot help but affect work and relationships. It can change us for the better.

Through music, this is possible. Through the right approach, it's achievable. Through the right system, it's doable. Through a method where "everyone can play", the world can be a different place. Given the right tools, abilities and attitudes, where there is a safe environment of freedom and creativity, no judgment, a place where students can explore and learn from their failures, where success is experienced, and where learning is fun, we can tell "the untold story". Here are some of them.

Bernadette E. Ashby
San Jose, 2010

PUBLISHERS NOTE

Delight. It's a word we don't use much in everyday conversation. That's unfortunate. Because, even as adults, we still want the enchantment of delight in our lives.

> For most of us, originality is at the
> heart of our delights.

> Imagination...

> Inspiration...

> Creativity...

> Growing and building, alone or in community...

In a culture where so much of our time is structured for what we must do, we rarely consider what we might delight in doing. When our lives are filled with rush and stress, we don't choose creative forms of relaxation. For example, we may love music, but few of us play. Why?

Perhaps because we have been persuaded it can't be done. We don't have the time, or the talent, or the training. We have tried before, but have become frustrated and given up.

Take heart! There is a transformation sweeping around the world. A new way of seeing music. It's not a rhythmic style or performance technique. It's a way of looking at how we learn to play. The results of such a shift are astounding. Children can carry their creativity into adulthood. Adults have an effective way to 'change gears' after a long day. We all gain the confidence that comes from doing something well - that we love.

When I started working on this project with Bernadette Ashby, I knew nothing about Simply Music. Since that time I have learned a great deal – more importantly, I have seen the ongoing effects of a steady supply of delight; stress relieved, confidence raised, joy renewed.

Bernadette is uniquely qualified to create this book. As an educator, business owner, homeschooling parent, and writer, she has seen and experienced many of the struggles we all face. She has collected stories which are encouraging, insightful, and invigorating. Through her approach to music Bernadette has changed lives. I am sure this book will do the same.

What would life be like if we all enjoyed a touch of delight each day?

Gail K. Efting
Sunnyvale, 2010

WHAT PEOPLE ARE SAYING...

Finally, I found Simply Music! After having taught traditionally for over thirty years, I could not know the joy and pleasure of helping students learn to play the piano for keeps. The method is more than "teaching" piano. It is a multi-faceted way for students to discover their musicality and to attain skills that will enrich their lives no matter their age or circumstance. And perhaps most importantly of all, I find myself a member of an incredible family of teacher/mentors who truly love and believe in what they do.

Lynn Frank, Simply Music Teacher
Lexington, North Carolina

§§§

I'm so happy at my advanced age to be playing the piano. I'm now able to compose songs from my brain to my fingers... to my delight!

Vera Barton, Student, Age 76
Agoura Hills, California

§§§

This is a wonderful music program and the results are astounding! Even if you don't consider yourself musically talented, this program is designed for you! It is easy to understand and easy to play a full repertoire of beautiful songs from a variety of genres. I also think this program could be a major breakthrough for children with a variety of cognitive delays and learning disabilities. I love the Simply Music approach.

Dr. Anne Margaret Wright, Licensed psychologist
and co-founder of Cyber Educational Consultants
Touro University International

Quotes from my kids last night: Ethan, "I love piano lessons." Connor, "I am gifted in music." It does my fatherly heart good to hear such enthusiasm. I promise you those two comments never came out of my mouth during my seven years of traditional lessons.

Doug Russell, Parent
Omaha, Nebraska

§§§

As a result of Simply Music, my nine-year-old son is not only playing the songs in his repertoire, he's improvising his own tunes, reading chord changes, and teaching himself new songs. And if he happens to be in a place with a potential audience, he's more than happy to sit down and play for them! Every aspect of Simply Music – technical or otherwise – keeps students engaged in performing music that's totally connected to their world.

James DiPasquale, Parent, Film Composer
Past President of the Society of Composers & Lyricists
Beverly Hills, California

§§§

Facing the challenges of autism, Simply Music has opened doors that we never dreamed would open. It is so difficult to put into words the impact that Simply Music piano lessons have had on our daughter and consequently on us, her parents. This way of learning seems tailor made for her. Hearing her play and watching her learn gives us hope that she will be okay in life.

Joe and Helen Morris, Parents
Lexington, North Carolina

I have seen a lot of music programs over the years. Some were fun. Some were clever. Some were thorough. Here's one that has it all. In terms of presentation, effectiveness, philosophy – you name it – there's nothing out there that compares at all.

Mary Pride, Publisher, Practical Homeschool Magazine

§§§

Simply Music has opened up the world of music making for our nine-year-old son in a way that we never could have imagined. My husband and I are conservatory-trained classical musicians. When we first attempted to teach our son piano using the traditional method of reading music, we were met with frustration and his eventual refusal to continue with lessons. Now, nine months later, he literally runs to play piano in the mornings before school.

Joan and Jeff Beal, Parents, Grammy Winner
San Francisco Opera Alumni
Agoura Hills, California

§§§

WOW! I was only looking for a few hints on the internet to help with teaching very young children to play the piano! I didn't expect to have my traditional piano-teaching-roots challenged to the core and turned on their head when I came across Simply Music. Pretty soon I realised there was no turning back. This program made complete sense. In fact I wanted my own kids to learn this way. Now I'm teaching this brilliant method to all my students.

Paul Chester, Simply Music Teacher
Cheltenham, South Australia, Australia

I began my piano lessons in Russia and then went to music school for seven years. Everyday was a struggle because I had to practice for an hour playing boring etudes and complicated musical pieces which I hated. When I graduated I didn't touch the piano for one year! When we started Simply Music for my son, I was very skeptical. I thought he would last maybe a month. It's been almost two years now and he loves playing. His repertoire is greater than mine even after studying seven years in music school!

Yana Gafouri, Parent
Corte Madera, California

§§§

I always had a yearning to play the piano and envied those who could. I have many happy memories of family sing-a-longs around the piano. I can't believe my luck in finding Simply Music. I'm not sure what I expected and have never learnt music. I love music and feel stimulated by learning the Simply Music way. I am sure my memory has benefitted and will in the future.

Jane Pease, Student, Age 62
Hawthorn, Victoria, Australia

§§§

This revolutionary technique allows the student to better recognize the forms of music without the mystery and enables them to more quickly participate in the joy of creating and performing. This isn't a short cut to understanding music, it's a straight line.

Marc Bonilla, Parent, Emmy Award Nominee
Professional Musician/Composer
Winnetka, California

COMING HOME

The Story of One Man

The Beginnings

Neil Moore's eyes light up when he talks about Simply Music. He sees a revolutionary approach for introducing students to the piano. Students initially skip the music reading process and repetitive scales and use a completely new method, learning how to play well-known and great-sounding music right away. "The idea is to *play* the piano, not to *learn* the piano," Moore explains. The program is nothing less than a breakthrough in self-expression. "I honestly believe we can alter the culture of music education and create a new direction, an entirely new possibility."

The beginnings of Simply Music are so intertwined with Moore's life, it's impossible to pinpoint the idea's exact inception. A native of Australia, Moore was the youngest of five children born to parents who loved music. "My dad was a singer; he loved Streisand and Big Band music. My mom loved Ella Fitzgerald, Ray Charles, Oscar Peterson. There was always music playing in our home, and whenever we were all in the car, we would sing and harmonize songs. It was a very musical experience. It was very important to my parents for the children to have an opportunity to learn music. "

Each of the four Moore boys began piano lessons at age seven. Their mother made them each practice twenty minutes a day, so music filled the house. Moore, the youngest, was exposed to all of it from infancy. His affinity for music was evident from those earliest days. His mother tells how, as an infant, he'd roll to the radio and "just lie there, listening."

By the time he began studying piano, music was a passion. From the beginning, however, young Neil never connected the written musical notes on the page to what was being played. Instead, he heard music and visualized it in his own unique way. He'd watch his teacher play and then reconstruct what he heard. "I would hear melodies and see them as shapes and patterns. It was like having a musical Lego™ kit." He faked reading the sheet music during piano lessons. "I was able to play and I was playing well, so during lessons I just stared at the page – not reading a single note – and I would just play the piece and think I was fooling my teacher." But of course he wasn't. Years later, Moore's mother told him the teacher would come to her to report that Neil wasn't reading at all. "My mum said, 'Look, he's playing and he's playing well, so just let him go.' Our parents only wanted music to be a pleasure to us. They always imagined it would be a great hobby and a great love to have, so they were very relaxed about it."

By the time he was twelve-years-old, he could hear a song on the radio by a group such as the Beatles and play it. "Not only would I work out the melody, I'd work out the chords and listen to Paul McCartney's bass line and I'd work that out and it became a multi-layered relationship that I had with the piano. I had a way of teaching myself that was perfectly natural to me." He also taught himself drums well enough to play in a band, but that never

2

overshadowed his passion for piano. "It was my single biggest love," he says. "It was a companion."

By age fifteen, he was playing a repertoire of classical, pop, blues, jazz, ballads, accompaniments and was composing some of his own music and arrangements of popular pieces he liked, "and could not read a single note of music." Over the next fifteen years, he had lessons with numerous teachers in an attempt to go back and learn to read, but it was very frustrating. Some teachers tried starting with basic piano pieces such as <u>Mary Had a Little Lamb</u> and what was the point of that? Others tried to layer the math and theory of music on his self-taught, advanced techniques, but it was too complicated. "I didn't have a clue what I was doing, mathematically," Moore admits. Later, however, that frustration would serve him well. He learned a lot about what doesn't work in music education.

As an adult, Moore continued playing, never considering music as a possible career. "I always had this yearning for music, but I didn't feel like I had the right to pursue that," Moore says. "Everyone in my family was self-employed – for generations. That was the thing to do." Music was a hobby, not something stable enough to support a family.

And so he followed the family entrepreneurial blueprint. It wasn't enough. "I owned restaurants and was good at what I did, but I wasn't happy," Moore says. "I had restaurants that were well known and well-regarded – they were successful – and I was an unhappy person. I couldn't quite rationalize that. I remember thinking, I've been blessed with a beautiful wife, beautiful children, a great family, a lovely home, great cars, I have a great business… I *should* be happy."

Moore's plan was to make as much money as possible in business, so he could retire early and in some way pursue music.

But the dream always felt so distant. "I just felt deeply unchallenged and like something was wrong," he explains. "I can see now that I wasn't honoring my calling."

In the late 1980s, the worldwide stock market fiasco left the Moores in financial ruin. Neil watched as everything – cars, furniture, electronics, their home, pianos – were repossessed, carted away or sold off. "I have very vivid memories of my children opening the refrigerator and there being no food in the house and I had no money to go out and buy any. It was a phenomenal and humbling experience." The dichotomy of it all was just as unmistakable. Losing everything gave him a powerful perspective 'on the nothingness' of material wealth. "I remember the day the tow truck pulled up to take away my wife's Volvo and my Mercedes and I'm standing at the front of the house. There was just this moment of realization that they were taking *nothing*," he says emphatically, "that nothing that they were taking really mattered."

"I'd been working hard in pursuit of money to eventually pursue my love, when what I really needed to do was pursue that love and have faith that everything else would be taken care of," he says. "In a dialogue with God I said, 'I don't know what You want, other than I believe You have a plan for me and I know it to be in music.' Right there and then, I vowed to pursue what I was called to do."

Out of the blue, a friend of a friend asked Neil and his wife, Cathy, to be partners in a restaurant with him. While Cathy Moore did most of the work with advice here and there from Neil, Neil returned to school to fill in his technical gaps in music. He was in the process of trying to borrow a piano when he met a man who was recruiting teachers for a new music reading program. Moore decided to give it a whirl and quickly discovered he was a natural teacher. In less than a year, he had one-hundred-and-twenty students and was training other teachers in the program. He was offered a partnership in the company. Soon after, he was asked to go to the United States to introduce the program there.

The idea for his own music program arose when someone in Sacramento asked Moore if he thought he could teach an eight-year-old blind boy to play the piano. Traditional sheet music was out of the question so Moore decided to try to reach him using methods he'd discovered as a child. He explained the layout of the music on the keyboard in terms of shapes and patterns. The child seemed to be getting it. The shock came a few months later when Moore learned the boy had also begun teaching the songs to his four-year-old sister, who also was blind.

Moore had an epiphany. "It was a profound moment," Moore recalls. "I began to think, 'I wonder what would happen if I taught all young children this way. No reading, no theory, no math. Just playing.' At that time I thought of it almost like music pre-school, a forerunner to this reading-based music program I was teaching."

So he began experimenting with other students when the unexpected occurred. Without exception, they produced better results and played more easily than Moore's more advanced students. Within about ten weeks, beginning students typically were playing six to ten songs. "I thought, 'I wonder how far I can take this?'" he says. He came to believe that much of the struggle with traditional programs was a result of the insistence that beginners work from a printed page. That, Moore likes to say, "is like expecting children to read and spell before they first learn how to talk."

Over the next several years, Moore immersed himself in codifying his ideas into a complete curriculum. In 1998, he opened five Sacramento-area piano schools to demonstrate the remarkable results being achieved by the new 'playing-based' program he called Simply Music. The instructors he initially recruited for training included classically trained piano teachers. Others were qualified guitar and flute teachers, whom Moore trained to deliver his Simply Music method. A few were accomplished, professional musicians with no teaching experience. Some of those that Moore trained had never before had piano lessons. And yet all of the teachers easily duplicated Moore's stunning results with students.

"We just started to see incredible things," Moore says. "It was unbelievable. Children were coming and having lessons and going home and teaching their parents to play. Grandparents were having lessons and teaching their grandchildren to play. Homeschool families would come. One of the children would have the lesson and then go home and teach all of his brothers and sisters. It was just a fantastic thing to see."

Moore's research shows that students are drawn to Simply Music for four reasons:

♦ the quality of the music they learn right away
♦ the quantity of music they learn to play
♦ how quickly they learn
♦ how easily they learn.

Moore's Simply Music method is based on the premise that everyone is naturally musical. With this as its basis, the program uses a 'playing-based' approach, which translates pieces into concepts that unfold directly onto the keyboard. The unique concepts are simple and easily understood by children and adults. The method includes a body of music covering blues, contemporary, classical, ballads, jazz, accompaniment pieces, composition, and improvisation. After establishing a strong basis in playing, students easily progress through Simply Music's non-traditional approach to music reading.

From these beginnings, Simply Music is now taught at close to five hundred locations throughout the USA, Canada, Australia, and New Zealand. Plans are underway to launch into Europe, Asia, and other parts of the world. Educational inroads are also being made into special needs areas such as Autism and Tourette's Syndrome. As more people and associations see the need for our culture to be musically expressed, Simply Music as an organization is preparing to meet this need, creating a higher profile and public awareness of what it has to offer.

Moore believes the Simply Music method will revolutionize the way music is taught. "This method is a breakthrough in music education. This is a program for the masses. It's for anyone who's ever wanted to experience playing music," he says. "I want people's first experience with music to be, 'I love this. I want to do this for myself. Why? Because I can do it and it's fun. I *am* musical...'"

"We have to create a new way of thinking about music. We have to redefine what being musical means. Simply Music is about creating a new framework that says, 'All mankind is profoundly musical and everyone can express themselves musically.' I see this as ushering in a new era."

Moore is finally doing what he felt called to do. "To my DNA, I know that this is what my life was about," Moore says. "I'm experiencing a spiritual and emotional satisfaction that's on a whole other level. I've come home."

§§§

CHAPTER 1

BREAKING BARRIERS

Why this Breakthrough Method Works

By Bernadette E. Ashby

San Jose, California

Bernadette E. Ashby received her Master of Arts in Education, with an emphasis in Curriculum Development, and a Master of Arts in Religion. She is a credentialed teacher in the state of California and has taught all age levels, including as an adjunct professor at Trinity International University. Her favorite students are her three homeschooled children. She chooses to use her background in education to teach others about the benefits of a new way of learning.

A Changed Life

Every week, it's the same. This little girl greets me with a warm hug and then proceeds to feel everything on my body from head to toe. And I let her. "I'm wearing a green shirt and black boots. Here's a heart charm on my necklace," I explain. I take her hand in mine and we travel through the maze of familiar furniture until she reaches my piano. Lessons commence. "Jenna, that was fantastic! You're doing a great job. Do it again." I smile as she pushes down the piano keys. Jenna is my ten-year-old, blind, and deaf student.

Never in my wildest dreams did I imagine myself teaching such a delightful child, let alone managing a piano studio of over sixty students. How is this even possible? After all, I lacked experience, since I really only started to *play* the piano as an adult. I've been on an amazing journey, living out a dream I never thought possible. I pinch myself on a daily basis! Dreams do come true. I can attest to that.

In my adult mind, it was impossible to think that I could play the piano, let alone teach. As a child, I remember listening to my friends playing songs like Für Elise by Beethoven and Linus and Lucy by Vince Guaraldi. I wanted to do that, too. I sensed that something was missing in my life – something musical about me that I needed to express. It was as if a volcano was watching, waiting, welling up in preparation to erupt.

One day, my dad came home with a record player, an invention that played vinyl records. At last, I could listen to my favorite music at will; Jackson Brown, The Beatles, The Eagles. I even enjoyed my father's choice of music. He would play songs like The Blue Danube, The William Tell Overture, or the theme song from 2001, A Space Odyssey. I loved music! Music moved me and music was waiting to come out.

As a child, my parents were generous enough to rent me a clarinet for school lessons. The sessions lasted about a month before I quit – then I tried the piano. My first piano teacher was a professional musician. After about a month, I told my parents I didn't want to learn anymore. My determined parents, whose Asian background included nurturing their children's musical talents, tried another strategy. They took me to another teacher who taught with less structure. This seemed to work for a few months before I quit again. Consequently, I really believed that I would never be able to play. I gave up the idea.

But music kept needling me – an inner voice telling me that music was within me. During my college years, I hired a teacher and took lessons for a few months. I was really hoping that this time lessons would work, that my dream of playing the piano would be fulfilled. But after a few months of lessons, I quit once more. I wanted to learn, but within a few piano lessons my enthusiasm waned. All I really wanted to do was *play* the piano. My futile attempts led me to believe I was a failure at piano playing – that in my lifetime, I had to accept that my dream would never come true. I was sorely disappointed by what I assumed to be my lack of musical ability. Years went by and I studied and earned my Masters degree in Education. I love teaching and enjoy pouring into my student's lives. But music would always be a love for me.

I vowed that when my children were old enough, they would take piano lessons. My dream changed. If it wasn't possible for me to play, I would live vicariously through my children's experience of playing the piano. At a homeschool conference, I happened upon the Simply Music booth. They were advertising their Australian Breakthrough Piano Method. Beginning students were playing blues, classical, accompaniment, and contemporary music from their very first lessons. I stood there in disbelief. My experience told me that there could be no such method! I even told the gal working at the booth that it wasn't possible. Certainly, in my training as an educator I never saw anything like this. But hope is an incredible motivator – a friend to the downtrodden. I revisited the booth three times that day asking myself, "Is this really possible?" Finally, at the end of the day, the gal told me, "There's a money back guarantee if you are not satisfied." I had nothing to lose.

I intended to teach my children through the Simply Music method. But I discovered that *I* was able to play. I loved it, couldn't get enough! The musical seed that was planted deep within me was beginning to sprout. I was determined to learn more. Since the self-paced curriculum only went so far, I called the Simply Music headquarters to find out how I could expand what I knew. Neil Moore, the founder of Simply Music, told me, "In order to learn more, you need to become a teacher." I thought to myself, "Can it really be possible to be a teacher with my limited experience?" I laughed at him, "That is ridiculous!" I had only been playing the piano for two months. In a matter-of-fact voice, he repeated his comment.

Eventually, the overwhelming need to express myself musically overcame the doubts about becoming a Simply Music teacher. I made the decision to enter the world of music and it has never been the same. Simply Music overcame the many years of failed attempts and broke through the concrete wall of my misconceptions, a belief that said, "I will never be musical."

As an educator, I've been trained to assess learning strategies and philosophies that would help in the educational process. As a parent, I am looking for the best educational opportunities for my children. As a homeschool mom, I am looking for curriculum that is flexible and 'outside of the box'. I am constantly assessing the value of any approach. Why does this system work? What's different about it? Why would anyone consider using it? Why would anyone want to teach using this method? The same questions that I have asked in the past, I now asked about Simply Music. Through the years since, the answers have unfolded before me as a student and teacher of the Simply Music program. I've experienced these answers first hand.

Now, the voice within no longer needles me. The dream which was dormant in me for so long has taken flight through Simply Music. Because of this remarkable breakthrough piano method, people can live out their desire to express themselves musically. My dream has become real! Now, it is my heartfelt desire to share with others the joy that music has brought me. I believe there are those out there in the world who have the same questions I asked. This book answers those questions.

What is a Breakthrough?

Breakthrough – an interesting word. Often associated with a new promotional fandangle, 'breakthrough' conjures up visions of 'the latest and the greatest'. Webster's dictionary defines it as, "an act of overcoming or penetrating an obstacle or restriction." So what, exactly, is that "obstacle or restriction"?

The Simply Music premise states that everyone is deeply and profoundly musical. Music is not limited to the talented or gifted. We see it in the natural rhythms of children when they are coloring a picture or the rhythmic pace at which we walk on a daily basis. Even our speech exemplifies a sense of musical rhythm and pitch. Around the world, other cultures reveal through their instrumentation and vocalization that all people are musical. Nevertheless, some of us believe that we are not. But the Simply Music message conveys that each one of us is innately musical and that everyone should have the opportunity to express themselves in this way.

So, what is the "obstacle or restriction" that Simply Music is 'breaking through'? It is breaking through the existing mindset about musicality, who's capable of playing and who isn't, who's capable of teaching and who doesn't.

Simply Music changes the way we think about how we learn with holistic hands-on experiential learning, immediate musical self-expression, and social playing. Simply Music opens musical doors for the masses to access piano playing in a way that has never been done before. Because of this, it is altering the face of music education altogether.

Learning a New Way of Learning

An Australian Simply Music teacher came to the U.S. and stayed with me for a few days. She was new to the Simply Music program, but much more experienced in piano playing than I was. She asked me to teach her a few things.

I took her hands in mine and began to explain the pattern of the right hand of a song. Then I showed her what to do in the left hand. Slowly, using the resources from Simply Music, we brought both hands together. Within a matter of a few minutes, she was playing a beautiful classical piece without the written music in front of her. Her hands began to tremble and she began to cry. "Did I do something wrong to upset you?" I asked. "Oh, no." she replied. "It's just that I never learned how to play this way before."

We talked about what that meant for her, how learning in a new manner brought out such powerful feelings in her; patience, love, lack of fear, lack of rigidity when compared to how she learned as a child. Unmani had taken traditional lessons for ten years.

Like Unmani, most piano students learn how to play the piano through traditional means. Usually, learning up to seven different 'musical reading languages' at the same time is one of the hurdles that traditional students need to overcome. Proficient music reading requires these seven different skills; learning the languages of notes, rhythm, dynamics, lyrics, fingering, pedaling, and order. There is also a focus on technique. Imagine, if you will, learning Spanish, French, Swahili, Portuguese, Mandarin, German, and Japanese concurrently. If you tried simultaneously learning these musical languages, how long would you work before you quit? For many the experience becomes a *negative* one. It can be overwhelming.

I tell my students that I'm going to teach them a new way of learning. I have my students imagine that they are wearing a fishing vest with lots of pockets. We actually call it a 'musical vest'. We fill their pockets with musical tools that make learning to play the piano simple. One concept that I teach through Simply Music is the idea of a 'Single Thought Process' (STP), designed to help students break down and distill music into micro-events. The student is concentrating and mastering only one exercise at a time. Repetition creates a neurological pathway in the brain. This kind of step-by-step thinking process makes it easier for skills to be developed. The exercise is manageable and success is ensured.

I also teach the use of the 'External Speaker', speaking the instructions out loud. This deepens the learning process by adding another layer of sensory input and helps a student to articulate and reinforce the components necessary to execute a piece. I use many tools. Some of the other tools I use include; 'sentences, patterns, shapes', the 'Life Coach' (the role of the parent or caregiver, who plays a critical part in the student's accomplishments), the 'Play List', 'Navigating through Long Term Relationships', 'Fragmenting', 'Mapping', and 'Controlling the Events'.

Through metacognition, the awareness of how we are thinking about something, Simply Music provides a life skill of learning how to learn. The tools absorbed through the Simply Music program contribute to successful learning at every lesson. These skills can be carried over to other areas of life. Thus, Simply Music piano lessons become a *positive* experience in which the student can absorb more. Learning takes place more easily. It becomes a new way of learning.

Hands-on Experiential Learning

Rachel, a student of mine, was having great success with the Simply Music method. Within three years, she had become a 'self-generative' musician. She could play a large repertoire of songs in a variety of musical styles. She was comfortable with reading music, playing in the accompaniment style, composing impressive music, improvising her songs, and still loving to learn. It was no surprise to me when she told me that she had aspirations to become a professional jazz musician. Through Simply Music, she had been inspired to pursue a career as a professional musician. Simply Music provided her with a broad-based musical foundation so she could pursue a higher-level of music education. This is the result of Simply Music's 'holistic experiential music learning approach'.

What is this holistic music approach? If we learned music as we learn language, then the process would be natural. Children absorb language as part of their everyday lives. When a young child is learning a language, we don't require them to read a book, we allow them to mimic our speech. Over time, ambiguous expressions become clear words, words become sentences, and sentences become conversations. All of a sudden they are talking. Learning is organic and the child's effort is productive. The Simply Music method uses the same approach.

When a new student takes Simply Music lessons, the student learns the piano 'hands-on'. Educational research has shown that experiential learning is valuable and effective. This experiential 'hands on' approach has Simply Music students playing songs right away. The teacher establishes shapes and patterns into the student's hands, away from the piano, until they clearly know what to do. When they understand what to do, they play. Theory is interwoven throughout the learning process of functional piano playing. The student's personal musicianship grows as they experience practical learning. And at the same time, it's fun.

The more aural, kinesthetic, and visual the learning process, the more the information is retained. The multi-sensory approach of Simply Music and the Student Home Materials accesses the sensory gateways. The Student Home Materials includes a DVD which reviews the lessons, CD of the songs, reference books, and a piano pad. Through the help of these tools and the multi-sensory input, the student moves toward becoming a self-generative student – taking ownership of their own musicianship. This allows them to play, read, compose, and improvise on their own.

As with language, experience playing music is the best foundation for reading music. Prior to reading music, Simply Music students build a repertoire of over thirty, forty, fifty songs. Then, reading is introduced. I teach students how to write notes and rhythm as preparation for reading music. Writing music first is what differentiates the

Simply Music reading program from other music reading programs. I integrate writing rhythm and notes together in lessons until it becomes natural to the student. The student's base tools are established. Within a couple of weeks, students are reading songs they have learned from their playlist. Students are immediately successful with reading music since they are already familiar with these songs. They have the ability to 'reverse engineer' what they know in their hands on to the page and vice versa. This makes reading productive.

One day a student came in and asked me if we could learn a certain song together in her group. We were just learning how to read music. She pulled out a piece of sheet music called <u>Pavane for A Dead Princess</u> – a beautiful, sophisticated classical piece. I sincerely replied, "Honey, I think that might be a little too difficult to learn at this stage." She looked at me funny. I was confused. Then I curiously asked her, "Can you play this song?" She smiled and nodded her head. She proceeded to sit down at the piano bench and played the first page beautifully. I was astounded! At that moment, I realized the power of the Simply Music reading program. I also realized the power of experiential hands-on playing. If it weren't for her experience of playing, reading could have been a prolonged, slow process. Because she knew her repertoire of songs, she could access and read them promptly. This gave her triumph in the reading process and a desire to read more music.

Hands-on experience with a variety of genres and creative playing are also part of the Simply Music experience. Many of us don't aspire to perform at concert level playing. Many people want to just sit down and experience the joy of playing the piano. Simply Music students' exposure to a variety of songs includes blues, jazz, accompaniment, contemporary and, obviously, classical. This exposure will give the student the freedom to follow a particular bent toward a certain style of music. Because they are not required to do all their work in one specific genre first, they can more easily enjoy them all. This encourages their love for all music. From their first lessons, Simply Music stimulates creativity. It opens up the world of composition, improvisation, and arrangements. These skill-sets give rise to innovative piano playing. Rachel, who wanted to become a jazz pianist, has since moved to the next level of her piano playing. By nature, jazz requires a very high level of creativity and improvisation. Simply Music engaged her desire and gave her the ability to fulfill it. She is still pursuing her dream to become a professional musician, practicing four to six hours a day. As her first teacher, I am extremely proud of what she has accomplished through Simply Music.

This ability to create and improvise is consistently true for continuing Simply Music students. The Simply Music Student Assessment Chart compares the skill level of a third year traditional student and a third year Simply Music student. This comparison records a heightened level of innovation and holistic knowledge base for Simply Music students. It is exciting to see the possibilities.

Immediate Musical Self-Expression

Anthropologists study cultures in which singing or playing a musical instrument is an everyday experience for everybody. Music may be as simple as sticks clacking together or as complex as a heavy syncopated drumbeat. People gather together and play, experiencing the fullness of music without fear, without the expectation of having to be an 'expert'. It is common. It is expected. Everyone plays.

Student Assessment Chart

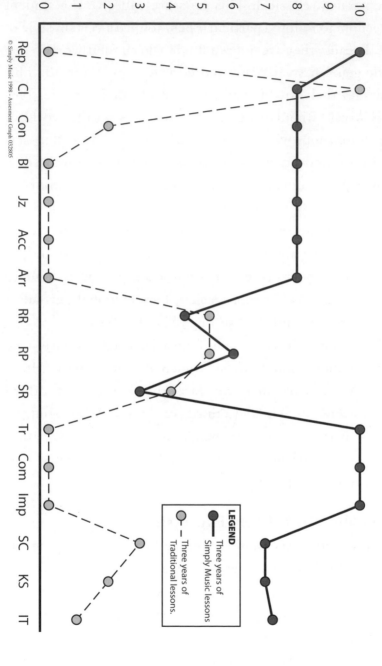

LEGEND

●— Three years of
Simply Music lessons

○-- Three years of
Traditional lessons.

Rep Cl Con Bl Jz Acc Arr RR RP SR Tr Com Imp SC KS IT

0 1 2 3 4 5 6 7 8 9 10

19

STUDENT ASSESSMENT LIST

1. Repertoire (Rep) - The size and diversity of the body music that can be played at any time, at any piano or keyboard, without the need for written music.

2. Classical (Cl) - Experience playing this style of music.

3. Contemporary (Con) - Experience playing this style of music.

4. Blues (Bl) - Experience playing this style of music.

5. Jazz (Jz) - Experience playing this style of music. This includes knowing the common array of jazz-style chords as well as how to read and use Lead Sheets.

6. Accompaniment (Acc) - Experience with, and the ability to read contemporary chord symbols, and play these in an accompaniment style while playing along with another instrument or vocalist.

7. Arrangement (Arr) - Experience with, and the ability to play additions (enhancements, developments, and variations) on an established composition, including the ability to selfgenerate these additions.

8. Reading Rhythm (RR) - Experience with, and the ability to accurately read and replicate rhythm as written on the page.

9. Reading Pitch (RP) - Experience with, and the ability to accurately read and replicate pitch as written on the page.

10. Sight Reading (SR) - The ability to accurately and immediately play on the keyboard, in a musical fashion, that which is written on the page.

11. Transcription (Tr) - Experience with, and the ability to hear music (whether notes and/or rhythm) and accurately write it on the page.

12. Composition (Com) - Experience with, and the ability to assemble melody, harmony and bass lines into an original composition.

13. Improvisation (Imp) - Experience with, and the ability to spontaneously assemble notes and chords into melodic and rhythmic phrases.

14. Scale (Sc) - A knowledge of the formula for creating scales, a knowledge of and experience with their structure on the keyboard, and the ability to physically navigate the scales and scalepassages with practical, comprehensive fingering.

15. Key Signature (KS) - A knowlege of and experience with the various major and minor keys, and their respective sharps and flats.

16. Integrated Theory (IT) - A practical, hands-on relationship with and knowledge of music, including its form, the theory behind its structure, the ability to identifying and name chords, scale and scale-passages, keys and progressions etc., with a given piece of music.

The beauty of the written form of music is that it can be recorded and preserved. But, written music can create additional limitations. For example, it can be assumed that those who cannot read music cannot play music. We are less 'musically expressed' in this culture because of the requirement to read the written form. Most of us believe that we cannot *make* music if we cannot *read* music.

We tend to believe that teaching music requires 'the basics'; reading, use of pneumonics, perfecting scales, developing excellent posture and finger position, fluency in the math of rhythm, working with metronomes – that all are necessary to produce skilled musicians. This is a common experience for a beginning piano student. The page dictates what to play. Rhythm is treated as a math because of the counting. And the focus is often on technique. Playing is analytical and 'receptive' in nature - the teacher or the page is telling the student what to do. After a couple of years of learning how to play the piano this way, students can often become quite frustrated. Many ultimately quit. Most importantly, they may lack self-expression – the ability to put themselves into a piece of music to make the song their own – because they have been trained to treat music as a regimented system. It can take years of study before a student feels comfortable enough to discover and explore self-expression.

But what would it feel like to walk up to a piano and be able to sit down and play music that you love with freedom, creativity, and sensitivity? Wouldn't it be wonderful to be able to play more than twenty, forty, sixty fantastic songs or more from memory? What if you could create a song at the 'spur of the moment'? What if you could play for your enjoyment and for the entertainment of others? These experiences are common among Simply Music students.

When my students see a piano, they are drawn to it like a vortex sucking them in. Their intimate connection with the piano allows them to be self-expressed. This self-expression is revealed through the way they play. Music becomes an emotional experience for them, speeding up, or playing with quietness and gentleness as appropriate. They are self-generating – pulling from their own personal resources and tools. They've learned how to play a song that is 'their own'. They also have the opportunity to compose and improvise songs even as beginners. This freedom creates self-expressed musicians who love to play and love to learn.

Consider the following comment from the parent of one of my students:

> *My son played his new composed piece for the talent show at school yesterday, and it was too beautiful for words. Several teachers and students complimented him and said they were deeply moved by his piece. The principal called me at home later in the day to say she was completely in awe, not only of his original composition, but the way that he played it. It would have given your heart wings to hear the praises.*

Social Playing

I greatly value the high level of parent participation in my studio. One mom experiences such joy watching her son perform for others that she seeks out opportunities for him to share his gift. She organizes visits for him and his fellow students to senior homes on a regular basis. He plays four to five different kinds of songs for the seniors without the written music in front of him. He plays effortlessly, with sheer enjoyment. It goes both ways. The audiences who delight in his playing show their appreciation beyond the intermittent clap by singing, tapping their feet, nodding their heads and exclaiming an occasional word of encouragement or, "Amen!" His fellow students are inspired, too. As they play, the common bond of music allows the young and old, even as strangers, to experience a camaraderie that wasn't there before. Piano playing provides the incredible opportunity to reach out to others. The students played. That mom made it happen. Simply Music made it possible.

In the past when people knew how to play the piano, others used to stand around the piano and sing. Everyone participated in the music. Today, there are other entertainments to draw our attention, but Simply Music can create an atmosphere where music can be shared. Generally, piano playing is an isolating event, hours of playing and studying alone. Often the end goal of piano lessons is performance; recitals, and competitions. After years of study, some students may have the opportunity to play as part of a band or ensemble. But do we have to study for years before we can perform? Simply Music strongly encourages and promotes social piano playing even for the beginning student. Music is a gift to be shared with others. The lessons in life are typically learned in a social environment. Why not piano? During the Christmas season, I pull out Christmas carols that even my beginning piano students can play. The Accompaniment Program of Simply Music provides students with the ability to read 'lead sheets' and play and sing Christmas carols with their family and friends. It's easy for them. The reality of family and friends gathering around the piano and singing is resurrected through Simply Music. My students' parents come back with enthusiastic reports that their children are leading others in song. Accompaniment playing engages others; it is a skill which cannot be developed unless there are others involved. Simply Music encourages this style of playing by providing students a full curriculum in this skill area. It contributes to social playing in a way that had been lost.

Simply Music students, also, gain experience within a shared lesson environment, promoting social playing. Surrounded by other students, the fear of playing is minimized because performing for others is normalized. Empowered, they gain confidence in their musicianship. In the educational arena, shared lessons would be termed 'cooperative learning', an activity that is highly regarded.

In shared lessons, three kinds of learning take place:

♦ see – observatory learning – where they observe what is going on

♦ do – participatory learning – where they play what they are learning

♦ teach – generative learning – where they are teaching others what they know.

This synergistic learning experience provides the basis for the power of shared lessons and their social implications.

Everyone Plays

After February 4, 1999, life would never be the same for Australian-born Teresa Killeen. While working as a nurse at a major hospital, she experienced a severe headache. On returning home, she collapsed from a stroke and subsequently slipped into a coma for two weeks. The doctors gave her parents the option to turn off her life support, but they believed that this was not the answer for Teresa.

24

She was twenty-nine-years-old, engaged to be married in a few months.

Because of her physical state, her relationship with her fiancé did not survive the enormous changes. On regaining consciousness through intensive rehabilitation, her comprehension and mobility was restored. Slowly with constant support from her loving parents, her physical rehabilitation allowed her to live independently. With her limited capabilities, Teresa wanted to do something to occupy her time. It was in this search that she and her mother met Joanne Jones, a Simply Music teacher.

Simply Music gave Teresa an unexpected breakthrough in her life. The stroke had caused brain damage particularly to the right side of her brain. Her parents wondered if she would ever be able to use her left hand and arm again. By bringing right and left hands into play, her brain revived old pathways and created new ones, enhancing healing. Teresa retrained herself how to use her left hand. In her own words, "It brought my brain back together."

Through Simply Music, she continues her rehabilitation. Joanne Jones comments:

Teresa is a wonderful testament to the success of this ground breaking approach to learning the piano. Yes, diligence and determination on the part of the student and the caregiver is an essential ingredient, but that we now have a program that truly maximizes the likelihood of any student having music as a companion for the rest of their lives in spite of impairments, is the greatest gift I can imagine as a piano teacher.

Why is Simply Music so important to someone like Teresa, who has experienced a life-altering stroke? Simply stated, Simply Music redefines who is capable of playing. Simply Music allows her to experience healing as well as her own musicianship.

What about someone who has special learning challenges? What about someone, like my student Jenna, who is blind and deaf? Simply Music opens up the possibility of a whole new musical world for those with special circumstances. Without Simply Music, Teresa's and Jenna's choices for experiencing their musical talents, learning how to play the piano, are extremely limited. The beauty of their stories is repeated in the lives of others. Simply Music insists on impacting the lives of many students and their teachers around the world, including those who have special challenges.

In addition to special needs students, Simply Music encourages adults of all ages to explore their musicianship through piano playing. The average age of traditional students falls between five and twelve years of age. With Simply Music, the average age is between five and ninety years. Simply Music is reaching out to adults who have always had a desire to play the piano, impacting their lives. Clearly, not only children want to play the piano. Adults want to play, too. Most adults just want to play recreationally, for entertainment. The adult market is an emerging, untapped constituency for piano teachers. Some of my Simply Music colleagues teach *only* adults. Everyone can play.

Redefining Who Teaches

A teacher is usually expected to have years of training and study in piano. Simply Music breaks through the notion that only experts can teach piano lessons. 5% of the Simply Music teacher body consists of novice and intermediate piano teachers, contributing their fresh excitement and passion of learning to their students. They have a great understanding of the new student's learning process because of their own recent experience. Some of the most successful Simply Music studios are taught by developing piano players.

Sonia Castro is one example. Being an educator in the Brazilian school system for twenty-six years, she came to the United States. She had hopes of pursuing her career, but never dreamed that she would be teaching piano. She started as a nanny for a couple of boys that happened to be taking piano lessons with Neil Moore. Since she couldn't afford lessons at the time, Sonia was happy to help the boys with piano practice. This allowed her to fulfill a life-long dream of playing the piano, but it became more than that – the experience changed her life. She went from being a nanny to being a Simply Music teacher. At first, Sonia was incredulous that she could do it, but with perseverance and support, she has proven herself to be successful. After eleven years of teaching, her average studio size is seventy students. Simply stated, Simply Music redefines who is capable of teaching.

My Breakthrough

The same breakthrough has occurred in my life. My journey as a Simply Music teacher began nine years ago and my life has never been the same. It is no coincidence that the very first song in the Simply Music curriculum is called

Dreams Come True. I've taught this song hundreds of times. Neil Moore had no idea how this song would impact my life and thousands of others.

I don't envy my childhood friends anymore – I can play Für Elise and the Linus and Lucy theme song. I now manage a full studio and have the privilege of teaching others how to play and express themselves musically. My students' parents are thrilled that their children are having fun and learning so much. It's a joy to watch my own children play better than I ever thought they could – three gifted musicians. I also never thought I could make such an incredible living working part-time. I have grown tremendously in my relationships and understanding of people as a teacher.

I am living out my dream to play the piano. And so much more. Music has become my companion for life. My dream has taken flight! I can fulfill my heart's desire to spend hours every day at the piano experiencing the pleasure of music. The beauty of this is that I have the rest of my life to do so.

This gift alone, for me, is enough to call Simply Music a breakthrough. But that's not all it is. As an educator, I am compelled to communicate the value of Simply Music to the world around me, to let others know that they are deeply and profoundly musical, to understand and experience the benefits of this unique way of learning. That's the purpose of this book. Simply Music can have an impact on a person's musical expression, as it has in mine. Simply Music brings joy and excitement back into learning, making piano playing fun, breaking barriers of the improbable. It truly is making it possible for "a world where everyone plays", a world where dreams do come true.

Dreams Come True
By Neil Moore

Sitting here with you,
Nothing much to say
Listen to my thoughts,
Pass the time away.

I like having dreams,
One for me and you,
Think I'll make my dreams come true.

§§§

Music is a key component in a child's well-rounded education. As an educator, I witness this on a daily basis. Students who participate in music not only perform better in math and other subject areas, but have better social behaviors and attitudes. I am impressed with Simply Music's approach to teaching the piano. Because my daughter experienced success by learning how to play a song during her first lesson, she felt confident, looked forward to her next lesson and had so much FUN!

Jerry Merza, Parent, Principal, Hellyer Elementary School
San Jose, California

CHAPTER 2

MY THOUGHTS

The View of a Ten-Year-Old

By *Aidan Menezes*
Balwyn North, Victoria, Australia

Aidan Menezes is a fourth grader at Belle Vue Primary School. Math is his favourite subject. He loves sports, reading, swimming, watching his favorite television shows, and enjoys playing the piano.

G'day

When I was eight-years-old, my parents decided that I should learn a musical instrument. I was not keen at all on learning the piano, but since my parents insisted, I thought I'd give it a go to please them and see how I like it.

So my parents were on the look out for a music teacher and one day my dad drove past the Simply Music studio close to where we live. We did not know of anyone attending the Simply Music program at that time. Dad called Kerry (my teacher) on the number advertised in front of the studio and he spoke to her. Kerry explained the Simply Music method to my dad and she invited us to attend a lesson. I was apprehensive at first, not knowing what to expect, but I found the lesson fun and easy at the same time. So my Dad had made up his mind – he was convinced that was the school for me! My parents were of the opinion that the traditional method of learning music would be too cumbersome for me and to get me interested in the piano they decided to give Simply Music a try.

I was enrolled in the Simply Music program and we have not looked back since. Two-and-a-half years on and Simply Music is still fun! Before I started piano with Simply Music I was unsure, neither motivated nor keen and definitely not confident at all, but now I enjoy playing the piano and am always looking forward to the class and to learning new things.

My parents bought an electronic keyboard for me to practice on at home as they did not want to buy an expensive piano, just in case I gave up and lost interest.

My Teacher

Kerry Hanley, my teacher, makes music fun and enjoyable. She is *very* good and teaches us so well. She has patience and she expects us to do our homework, as she does not like it if we have not practiced at least six days a week as this can slow the class down. Kerry gave me a very important tip on practicing my music. She told me to practice my piano 'at the same time' every day and this has now become a routine with me and has disciplined me to wake up, have my breakfast, and sit at the piano at 8 am daily for half an hour before leaving for school.

As I began to improve and enjoyed learning to play the piano, my parents decided to buy us a proper piano. It has strings and weighted keys. It is shiny and black and I take good care of it.

Why I like Simply Music

I would like to say that Simply Music is awesome because of

how many songs and variations of songs and compositions I have learnt (seventy one songs so far and I can play all of them) in the two-and-a-half years I have been with them. The songs vary and are very interesting. I look forward to new ones.

This method makes music easy for kids like me. The Simply Music program also allows us to have a huge repertoire of songs. A feature of the Simply Music program is the DVD and CD provided. Every level has a CD to refer to at home with all of the songs in that level. The CD plays all of the songs on a CD player so if you forget what a song sounds like, you just play that particular level's CD and listen to the song at home and it refreshes your memory! If you forget what you learnt at class, you play the DVD and the DVD explains what your teacher has done in the lesson. The person who has made this DVD is Neil, the founder of Simply Music.

Initially, we were a group of four, but slowly the girls dropped off and now we are just two boys in my class which starts at 7 pm every Wednesday. I look forward to my class every week and I have rarely missed a lesson. I am very committed to become a good pianist.

The relationship chart Kerry introduced us to taught me that sometimes we tend to go through ups and downs in our dealings, not only in music, but also in other areas in life.

How I Share My Gift with Others

Now that Kerry has taught me so many songs from the Simply Music program, whenever our relatives or friends come over, I can show off to them some of the songs I have learnt to play. They are very impressed that I can play so many songs now. I have also played a couple of blues tracks at my school assembly and all the children loved it a lot.

My friends at school learn the Suzuki method and the traditional method and they tell me how hard it is to learn chords! They also say that they learn classical songs and don't play the blues. I think I have it too easy.

I am not nervous to play in front of an audience and I like the concerts we have once a year when each of us students gets to play a piece in front of everyone. At the concert, I saw people of all ages perform at the Simply Music concert and to me it was amazing to see someone as old as my grandfather learning the piano the Simply Music way.

How I've Grown

I noticed that since I started Simply Music I have become more interested in all types of music and I have learnt to appreciate music and enjoy it! I am so glad that my parents made that decision for me to learn music.

I now have a better understanding of rhythm and a great sense of self esteem. I get to use my creativity and make up some compositions and that makes me feel good about myself.

I think that playing the piano has made my fingers so flexible. As a result, my handwriting has improved and I am thrilled about that.

I have disciplined myself to practice my piano daily and consistently at the same time. This has established a regular routine in my life. I realise that I need to *make the time* in order to achieve any goals in life.

How Simply Music has Affected My Family

By getting my dad and mum to sing, we spend quality time with each other and as a family. This seems to also brighten up our moods and entertain us. It makes us relax and unwind in the evening before going to bed.

My sister who is only four-years-old now will also be joining the same program soon. She listens to me play and has learnt to sing some of the songs. When my grandparents visit, they love to hear me play and are proud of me.

Why I would recommend Simply Music to Others

I would recommend Simply Music to everyone I know because:

♦ I find it teaches us to play music in a simple and easy way (as the name suggests).

♦ It is fun and keeps me interested all the time.

♦ We get to learn to play different *types* of songs.

♦ I have a very good teacher and I am very happy with the way she teaches me.

Thank you for giving me this opportunity to share my thoughts about my Simply Music experience.

§§§

The Simply Music program is an extremely clever way of learning how to play the piano. Just by starting off with no note reading at all in the beginning, by levels six or seven, you've shot all the way up to the big stuff in note reading! It's like BAM! You're sight reading like nobody's business! It's truly incredible. The results are amazing.

Travis Shaw, Student, Age 13
North Hollywood, California

CHAPTER 3

FINDING THE MUSIC WITHIN

The Heart, the Soul, and the Brain

By Dr. Walter E. Brackelmanns
Sherman Oaks, California

Walter E. Brackelmanns, MD is a board-certified psychiatrist and psychoanalyst, a Clinical Professor of Psychiatry at UCLA, and a mental health consultant to the Los Angeles Unified School District. He has worked for thirty years developing and teaching a unique and practical approach to couples therapy, both nationally and internationally. Dr. Brackelmanns has twice appeared on the Oprah Winfrey Show, has demonstrated his ideas in a five-part series on the Today Show, and has had his own nationally syndicated television program called Couples.

No Musical Talent

My name is Walter E. Brackelmanns. I am seventy-six-years-old, married with two children and three grandchildren. I am writing about my personal experience with the Simply Music program. I will tell you who I am, what I do, and what I believe. I will tell you about what led me to this program, how it has touched me, and some of my ideas about how music and this way of playing the piano organically affect the brain and the body.

I am the middle child of three children from a German immigrant couple that came to the United States in 1929. In Germany, my mother studied in a music conservatory and considered herself a pianist. Times were very tough after their arrival in New York because that was the year the stock market crashed. My parents struggled to survive economically. My mother taught piano to children to earn a little money. We always had a piano in the house. My mother desperately wanted her three children to learn how to play the piano. She forced my older brother, my younger sister, and me to take a few piano lessons. None of us took to it and none of us learned how to play the piano. I was convinced at that time that I had no musical talent and would never be able to play an instrument.

Even though we had no money, my father stressed the importance of education and strongly encouraged all three children to go to college. He also encouraged us to work because he had no money to give us. I knew I needed a scholarship to go to college, so when I got to high school I studied ten hours every day, seven days a week. I had a learning disability in elementary school and in those days no one knew about those things or what to do about them. I believed I wasn't as smart as the other children. Instead of giving up, I reasoned that if I studied harder than anyone else in the school I would be able to get good grades and a scholarship to college. I graduated with a 96% average.

Just to increase my chances for college, I did as many things as I could to enhance my record. I joined clubs. In the marching band, they loaned instruments to students and encouraged the students to learn an instrument well enough to play in the band. I picked the trombone and took some lessons from another student who was a skilled trombone player. I did not take up this instrument for the joy of playing or for the love of the instrument. I took it up and played it to improve my resume.

In retrospect, it is interesting to me that I had a similar experience with the trombone at age fourteen to eighteen as I had with the piano at age six. I never really got attached to it. It never captured my heart or touched my soul. It also, once again, reaffirmed for me the belief that I had no musical talent and could never learn or enjoy playing any instrument. I did get a scholarship to Rutgers University in New Brunswick, New Jersey, where I was a pre-medical student.

After graduating from college, I went to Georgetown Medical School, then interned at Los Angeles County Hospital in Los Angeles, California. After completing the internship, I joined the Navy and studied to be a fight surgeon. I was lonely and to take up some of my time, I took up the guitar with hopes that I would accompany it with my singing. I could not afford lessons so I bought a book and tried to learn how to play on my own. I struggled with this instrument for several years to very little avail. Eventually I stopped playing the guitar, but I did continue singing in the car and other places. The one instrument that continued to give me joy was my voice. I rarely sang for anyone other than myself and I was always my best fan. There was something missing, but I was convinced that I had no musical talent and I could never learn to play an instrument.

What's Missing?

I married and had two children. I have been married for forty-eight years. The years went by. I became an adult and child psychiatrist, a psychoanalyst, and couples therapist in private practice in California, USA. I became a Clinical Professor of Psychiatry at the David Geffen School of Medicine at UCLA, where I teach a model I conceptualized called Inter-Analytic Couples Therapy. At the present time, I am writing a book about my model of couple's therapy. Our daughter grew up and married and we now have three beautiful grandchildren. I was happy and my life was fulfilled, but there was still something missing.

About two years ago, my granddaughter, Rebecca, wanted to take piano lessons and was referred to a Simply Music teacher. My wife, Lois, was a gifted pianist as a child and won all the amateur awards you could win at the time in Canada. Lois is a graduate of the University Of Toronto Royal Conservatory Of Music. However, for many years she did not play the piano. About twenty-five years ago we bought a Mason Hamlin grand piano and some time after that she began to play again. When Rebecca started taking lessons, Lois became intrigued with this new method and decided to take lessons herself. She saw an ad for Simply Music that Susan Friedman had put in the newspaper. After one visit, she asked me if I would be interested in going with her to the lessons. I am very busy. I reluctantly agreed to go with no promise to continue.

The Heart and the Soul

For the very first time, I had a different musical experience. Through Simply Music, I understood that we all have rhythm and an ability to be musical. I felt like a 'fish dropped into water'. I have taken to this program and worked hard at it for most of the last two years. I continue to feel enthusiastic about the Simply Music Program and have made a passionate connection to the piano and to music. I, now, know, play, and sing about one-hundred songs. Here is the part about the heart. The piano takes me away from the world. It soothes me, comforts me, and fills my heart.

I get a joy from playing the piano that doesn't seem to compare to anything else I have done or am doing. I am eager to learn more. I am not sure why this has happened. I believe the most important factor is the Simply Music Program. I have to give a lot of credit to Susan Friedman, who is my teacher. She is skilled, knowledgeable, kind, patient, and creative, while at the same time adhering to the program as constructed by Neil Moore.

Also, there is my age and the stage of life I am in. This is a time where one tries to integrate, in a fulfilling way, all the past elements of your life. We try to fill in, if we can, things that have been missed or are incomplete. I believe we all try to find peace and happiness. If I took up the piano to become a concert pianist or a professional musician, I would wind up being very disappointed. However, I took up the piano to meet another creative part of myself. I took up the piano only for my own personal satisfaction. I took it up to soothe and comfort myself.

There are many aspects of this program that have touched me in very surprising ways. All my life I have heard that music touches the soul. I have never understood what that means. Since I began *playing* the piano (I want to emphasize the word playing), I feel like something special has touched my soul. I feel this strongly when I am playing and singing. Clearly, I have made a powerful connection to the piano which I was not able to make as a child. I did not make it to the trombone or the guitar. I am now convinced that music and the piano will always be an important and integrating part of my life. The only musical things that I have enjoyed before learning how to play the piano are listening to music, singing, and dancing. Because my soul has been touched by music through playing piano, it gives me the impetus to try new things that I have always wanted to do. My plan is to take up ballroom dancing with my nine-year-old granddaughter, Ally Rose, in the near future.

The Right Brain and Music

The last thing I want to talk about is the brain. Since we are now able to do functional Magnetic Resonance Imaging or fMRI, we can look at the brain and examine how it functions. When there is activity in the brain, the blood flow changes and gives us different heat patterns. We now know that the left brain is different from the right brain. Some researchers believe that we really have two brains, a left brain and a right brain. They have different functions and they each store different memories. The left brain is where reason and rational thinking resides. It is where language originates and where ideas and conceptualizing takes place. When we think about music we have to think about the right brain. The memory banks in the right brain are much larger than in the left brain.

There are four-hundred theoretical orientations in the world of psychology and each of these theories believes that it has the right answer. The current thinking in the new neuroscience is that the unconscious, humor, wisdom, emotions, and creativity all originate from the right brain. We now believe that what is important in healing emotionally troubled people is not the intellectual insight, but the *relationship* between the two people. What this means is that the right brain of the therapist connects to the right brain of the patient. This connection is largely nonverbal and non-conceptual. It is the emotional experience that we have with another human being that is healing in an emotional and organic way. By this, I mean the experience we have in a positive and negative way with others can actually cause organic changes to take place in the brain. Also, meditation, hypnosis, and mindfulness can increase the dendrites, and in some cases the number of cells in the brain.

We know that music is a very powerful way of reaching almost everyone emotionally. Different music touches different people in different ways. What I had not realized is that playing the piano could touch me so powerfully. It has been said that music is the universal language. It is not necessary to translate music from one culture or language to another. Everyone's right brain connects to music and the right brain does not require a formal language. What is intriguing about Simply Music is that, similar to human development where we learn to talk before we learn to write, in Simply Music we learn to play before we learn to read music. This process works directly on the right brain.

Many researchers, like Daniel N. Stern, a prominent psychoanalyst, believe that many of the nonverbal therapies, like music and art, are very much underrated and will in the future find a more prominent role in the treatment processes of many mental illnesses, like autism, schizophrenia, and bipolar illness.

One last point about the brain needs to be made. The brain is a little like a muscle, 'use it or lose it'. We now know that people my age should exercise their bodies and minds regularly. There are many ways to exercise your mind. Taking piano lessons is one of them.

As you can surmise from what I described about myself above, I never plan on retiring. I believe that everyone should always have a dream. I believe we should all continue to learn and grow. We have to age, but we do not have to grow old. I do not think that I took up the piano late in life. I think that I took up the piano at the right time in my life. In my work and in my life, I have learned many things. One of them is that we can do what we can do when we can do it and not one minute before. I encourage all of you who read this to pursue your dream, stay as healthy as you can, do good things for yourself, and above all, seek peace and happiness.

§§§

It's very important that my children have the opportunity to be resourceful and innovative in their thinking. The future problem-solvers of the world will be required to 'think outside the box' and be measured on how they improvise, adapt, and overcome. I believe the Simply Music method of musical training is a great way to reinforce these skills and will also help their discipline and desire to learn. They are given the freedom to explore and be creative and have fun during the process. Simply Music has been and continues to be a significant part of their lives.

Dave Rosa, Parent, Vice President of Product Development, Contributing Engineer and Inventor on Multiple Patents for the DaVinci Surgical Robot, Intuitive Surgical
Sunnyvale, California

CHAPTER 4

BRINGING MUSIC HOME

A Mother's Gift to Her Children

By Erin Lavelle
Thousand Oaks, California

Erin Lavelle is a thirty-something mom living in Southern California with her husband and two young boys. She has a career and is a full-time mom. While she has some musical experience, she had never played piano before.

You Start

Can you really embark on the musical journey when you think you are too far along in the path of life? Of course, the answer is yes, but why? While I still like to think I'm fairly young, I certainly was not born in the 1990's or 2000's like most Simply Music students. After all, I was around for the original <u>Star Wars</u> release in theaters. I may not be in my 'golden years', but I'm no child.

Like most parents, I was contemplating extracurricular activities for my children when I came upon Simply Music. In general, my parenting philosophy around extracurriculars is to

43

1) limit them and 2) make them fun activities the whole family can enjoy in our celebrations, traditions, and life. Music perfectly suited my objectives for extracurriculars and we are fortunate enough to have a piano. But, traditional lessons seemed like such a harsh introduction for very young children; one child, a toddler, and one child in early grade school. Simply Music was one of the few alternatives in my area. So, I explored it further.

"I really think your children are too young," commented the instructor, Mary Vita-Catama, after a phone call. I was so bummed. They are talented little kids and music can be made at any age, right? But she continued, "Would you consider taking lessons instead and then we can integrate the children as they are ready?" Thoughts began racing through my head – I'm a working parent with two small kids! I wasn't looking for an extracurricular for *me*! I haven't ever been able to coordinate my two hands to do anything!

Then I realized that a commitment like Simply Music should begin with me. I could bring music to my household immediately and teach the kids until they are ready to sit through a formal lesson. I started my musical journey one month later.

In the last year, I've moved through the first four levels of the Simply Music Program. Life is certainly busy at my house – two full-time careers with work-related travel. So the program has had to move at my pace. However, it's been the most exciting part of my year. I can now sit down at my piano and play for the kids, visitors, and my broader family. The kids even sing with me. They've made up new lyrics on occasion, broadening their rhyming/lingual abilities. In the past three months, my oldest son has joined me at lessons. He's just moved onto his third song. He knows them very well by ear, because of my own practicing, and he is learning to coordinate his hands to play them. He's gaining a lot of confidence being able to play for guests, usually Grandma!

A Big Gift

Each time my son takes a lesson, the teacher reminds him that I'm giving him a big gift by giving him piano lessons. At times, I sort of chuckle because I know he's thinking something like Legos™ might be better. She is right on so many levels.

By starting lessons myself, I've realized how refreshing it is to have an activity beyond work and kids. I'm not sure how many people are able to retain their hobbies after the compulsory work/kids/exercise loop, but as a society we've forgotten how important it is to truly enjoy a pastime. It's also very important for kids to see their parents enjoy activities of their own. It's a lot of pressure for a child to feel that his parents' happiness is riding on his accomplishments and hobbies. Of course, I love spending time with my kids and I can enrich my time with them. At the same time, I can do something musical for myself.

For my son, music is a huge gift. I don't envision him being a concert pianist or taking piano to a professional level. I do envision him playing music for school productions or playing while the family sings holiday songs. I want him to be able to turn on the radio and recognize even simple patterns. I want him to play piano for his own family some day. Through piano, he'll gain confidence and recognize his ability to achieve something special. And more immediate and tangible, he is learning the discipline to practice, how to listen to his teacher, and how to coordinate what he is seeing and hearing with his hands. Most importantly, all of this is coming with joy and fun through the Simply Music program.

Why Simply Music?

Simply Music starts with the best part of music – the songs. From day one, I was playing the first foundational piece with both hands! I didn't have to spend months doing chord exercises or learning to read notes and rhythms. The instant gratification of learning song after song is truly motivating for adults and kids alike. It's so obvious that learning is best done in a hands-on way. Rather than abstractly learning about staffs, note types, and chord progressions, each song is slowly building a new skill-set. Each foundational piece progressively trains the brain and hands to do more. The student is immediately connected with the piano and the music.

For my young children and even for me, Simply Music allows us to play through logical patterns without being confounded by letters, numbers, and symbols. Asking a four-year-old to get his finger on the 'E' and then play can be completely confusing. Then, layer on holding down this finger for one or two or three counts. It's all too overwhelming. Simply Music shows my son the patterns for a song and immediately he connects with the rhythm and notes. He's given clues to remember how his fingers work. Each week he builds his skill-set and does more. Eventually, all of the traditional chords and music reading come together when he is ready. In the meantime, he has a huge repertoire of songs and can really enjoy playing like he's supposed to!

The Musical Journey Continues On

I am looking forward to the continued learning for myself and my sons. I am so fortunate to have a teacher and a program that continues to fit into my life and my pace. Simply Music is truly a different and natural way of bringing music into my life and into my home.

§§§

I took piano lessons briefly at the age of seven-years-old. Now almost fifty years later, I felt I was too busy and too old to learn piano. The piano at my house was a silent testimony. I could not play a thing because piano music was a secret code to me. Then, I started Simply Music lessons. What a terrific system! I could play sweet little tunes immediately and the encouragement of my instructor was beyond my expectations. The reality of the Simply Music program hit me and took my breath away when I played Ode to Joy *for the first time. Thank you Simply Music for cracking the code and inspiring all to see the beauty of the musical world.*

Mary C. Wood, Student, Age: 56
Bellevue, Nebraska

CHAPTER 5

TRADITIONAL TO PLAYING-BASED

A Classically Educated Music Professional's Perspective

By Michele Favero-Kluge
Omaha, Nebraska

Pianist, Michele Favero-Kluge, is a traditionally trained professional musician. She performs regularly with the Omaha Chamber Music Society. As a performing chamber musician, she has performed in the United States and Europe and was on the faculty at the Omaha Conservatory of Music (1999-2004), where she developed the piano curriculum. When she is not performing, she instructs private piano students of all ages.

A Weary Journey

To all traditional music teachers that find you need to breathe new life into how you teach, Simply Music is certainly the way to go. At least it was for me. I came from a very traditional background.

Unlike my brother and sister who pursued concentrated music training, I wasn't really certain what I wanted for myself.

I obediently went along with whatever I was told to do regarding my music studies. As a child, the main focus of my studies was a classically-based repertoire. My first teacher studied at the Royal Academy of Music in London, England. My older siblings studied with him and were actively involved in competition and the rigors of piano. There were times later in my youth that I wanted to learn more popular music besides the classics. Ironically, my teacher allowed me to learn some of the Hooked on Classics pieces, piano reductions of Tchaikovsky ballets, and some of the music from the movie Chariots of Fire. As early as in the fourth grade, I fantasized about one day becoming a famous concert pianist. Eventually, the draw to music was too great. I was talented and had the fortune of having wonderful music teachers who inspired me. In junior high and high school, I became involved in school musicals, accompanying the choir, playing for the high school talent show, as well as solo piano works. Eventually, I went on to college and graduated from Southern Methodist University with a Bachelor's of Music in Piano Performance. From there, I studied in Budapest, Hungary with Balazs Szokolay at the Liszt Academy and in London, England with Alexander Kelly, chairman of the piano department at the Royal Academy of Music. In 1997, I graduated cum laude from the University of Nebraska at Omaha with a master's degree in piano performance. While there, I studied with composer/pianist Jackson Berkey of Mannheim Steamroller and co-creator of the Soli Deo Gloria Cantorum. For four years, I served as the Piano Department Chair at the Omaha Conservatory of Music. It has been an interesting road that I have taken and I have learned much. One of the most interesting things that I have learned is that traditional teaching methods are not for everybody!

After I left the conservatory, I was disenchanted with music education. First and foremost, I saw how brilliant students at the conservatory discontinued lessons due to boredom. I saw how politics motivated teachers to vie for students. I saw how the institution, whose piano department I started, charged people more tuition in order to create new piano programs for the department. What seemed to matter most was the bottom line, not the strain on people's budgets.

The last four years of my teaching career left me frustrated. I always hoped that there was a better way to educate people on how to play the piano, particularly when most people did not want to be educated in the *lofty* traditional way. Most people do not want to be concert pianists. So, why have we as music educators been teaching them the same way one would teach a concert-artist-to-be? That way of teaching is fine at a college level or for some serious middle or high school students, but the vast majority of students who want to learn how to play the piano would just like to be able to sit down at an instrument and enjoy playing for a few hours without their pieces being competition perfect. Where would music be if there had not been casual musicians who simply wanted to play in order to express themselves? Music would be a very boring place. For thousands of years, humans from all cultures and all walks of life have had a need to communicate through music. If music is innate and there are many ways to express it, why should there be only one way to teach it? These and other questions plagued my weary mind.

Breath of Fresh Air

Three years ago, I came across the Simply Music method because a local news channel was doing a series of Consumer Watch Reports on it. I quit teaching at a local music conservatory a year before and was again teaching music out of my home. Over the years, I've experienced the difficulties in acquiring traditional students and keeping them, so the report piqued my interest. I instantly felt curious and a bit threatened to think that there might be a better method out there that might ruin my business. All my years of study would be for naught. When I watched the news show, I was pleasantly surprised. The method seemed legitimate and I immediately became excited. I contacted the music teacher that was interviewed and traveled to her home. I was intrigued by everything she said. She seemed invigorated by her teaching and passionate about giving her students the best music education possible. Her excitement was a breath of fresh air. We spoke for over two hours. I thought to myself, "Why not take a shot and talk to Neil Moore, the creator of Simply Music, to see what he has to say?" I was very glad that I did for what he imparted to me was a renewed excitement of teaching.

Non-Traditional Concepts that Work

Coming from a traditional background, there is a profound sense of a 'right way' to learn and a 'wrong way' to learn. Traditional students usually go through competitions. But before they can even be considered, there is a very strict regimen of practicing scales, playing etudes, drilling passages, learning three to four pieces once to twice a year of differing styles, and memorizing one or two pieces by year's end. Finally, they need to perform the pieces in a competitive setting or recital, or both. Sight-reading, proper technique, and theory are generally expected to be included in the curriculum. Rhythm is taught as a math based on counting.

Although I was good at math, I struggled with learning rhythm as a math. I recall one day, a composition professor walking up to me and questioning me with regards to how I ever got accepted into music school. He could see that I was struggling with the rhythm. At that point, I had the fear of God put in me and I was determined to master rhythm, which eventually and gruelingly, I finally did. I believe that it need not have been so difficult for me if it had been explained in terms that I could understand and relate to naturally.

Because of my unpleasant experience with rhythm, I learned several ways to explain rhythm to my students. I realized that there was more than one approach to teaching such musical concepts. When I discovered the Simply Music approach, it seemed to make the language of rhythm much less complicated. Exercises that put rhythm into the hands and the body first before playing made so much more sense to me than just putting it into the fingers and counting out loud.

Another concept I learned from my first instructor was to read notes as intervals (distances) rather than just memorizing notes and their locations on the page. I am amazed at the number of adult students I have taught who have previous traditional experience. They were expected to memorize the note and its location rather than read the distance from one note to the next. The Simply Music approach uses the intervallic approach to note reading. It helps the student to understand the relationship between the notes on the page and the distances on the piano. Of course, the student is required to memorize locations on the piano and the printed page, but from there the student can find the location of other notes. Again, this made perfect sense to me.

While practicing scales and etudes, drilling, and studying different periods of music are all legitimate and useful to learning how to play the piano, certain aspects of musicianship are missing which were taught to most young musicians hundreds of years ago. These concepts are improvisation, composition, and accompaniment. Johannes Brahms and Johann Sebastian Bach are two of many such famous composers who were taught to do these very things. Most students will never become concert pianists, but many will be asked to accompany others in a school music performance, musical, or in the church choir. Unfortunately, many of these students can only play with the score in front of them. With the help of Simply Music, these foundational ideas have been given a renaissance and can be included into the Simply Music lesson time. Too many times in traditional lessons, the inherent message received from the teacher to the student is that the student interpret the music exactly from the page or play the piece exactly as the composer originally intended it to be played, but there is so much more to music than this. My husband, who is the Principal Violist with the Omaha Symphony, told me on several occasions that many of the musicians who come to perform pops concerts with the symphony are such amazing musicians. They cannot only play their instruments well, they can also improvise and arrange various musical styles on the spot. Through the Simply Music method this concept can be taught and fostered.

In the typical traditional settings, initial pieces are quite elementary and not very interesting. They generally consist of some sort of two-note black key piece using quarter note pulses. If the student stays with the traditional program long enough and is not bored, this can lead to a greater number of pieces consisting of more interesting material, varied rhythms and motives, and greater technical difficulty. The problem therein lies: if a student can withstand these initial elementary sounding pieces and drills, s/he can then climb to greater heights and work towards concert-level repertoire. This process takes several years before any of these things can be achieved so the student and/or the parents need to be very supportive and patient. The results are not achieved over night.

The Competitive Nature of the
Traditional Environment

Sometimes it is not the approach to music that burns out students, but the highly competitive nature of learning music. Students have and will always compare themselves to other students. That is human nature. There are times when this can make or break a student. I have a young student now who took a few years of traditional lessons before taking Simply Music with me. She became so fearful of making mistakes in lessons that she would get very upset and cry. Her prior experience of learning took all of the joy of studying music out of her. It took a while to regain her trust, but now after studying with me using the Simply Music method, she has blossomed. She exudes confidence at the piano and is not afraid to play in front of others anymore. Piano used to be drudgery for her. Now it is a wonderful form of self-expression for this student.

Not only can piano competitions and festivals be daunting and competitive for the student, but it is highly competitive for teachers, too. They are always comparing their teaching styles to those of other teachers. Teachers are constantly forced to be inventive and creative to keep students interested in their musical pursuits. They need to also make sure that they are teaching all of the theory, technique, and styles that are expected of reputable teachers. Sometimes this overzealousness can be detrimental to students. I cannot say how many times I have taught students who were forced into competitions and festivals. Every single last one of them hated it. Hearing their recollections of competition experiences and the stress of it all made me wonder why they continued studying at all. Although these experiences may separate the 'men from the boys', I also ask the question, "Are they really for young students who just want to learn to play an instrument and enjoy it?" When teachers or parents are willing to place their children in competitions, I believe this becomes an inadequate mode to make certain that students stay motivated for continued music studies. This mentality works for some, but not others.

Traditional Teacher to Simply Music Teacher

Why should instructors change to teaching the Simply Music method instead of reinventing their own style? Here are a few things to consider; in this day and age of our evolving Western culture, it is difficult to keep traditional students forever engaged in the study of music. Parents often want their children to dabble in this or that activity possibly because they did not have the opportunity themselves growing up. They live vicariously through their children. I feel that this is a mistake because the child often becomes a jack-of-all-trades and is unable to focus on one activity. Quite often, as I have seen in my own studio, a student encounters and overcomes a very difficult learning challenge. The parent then takes the student out of lessons because the parent thinks that their child is just not getting anywhere. I see the student's growth, but in spite of my protestations as a teacher to leave the child in lessons, the parents say, "We just need a little break and then we'll contact you in a few weeks." By that time it is too late and the student is lost, in spite of later contact with the parents. Many start lessons and then stop because another activity takes precedence over piano lessons or because parents do not have the resolve to support their child.

There are few serious students and generally many serious teachers. Even if a teacher is a gifted instructor, they may discover that there are not as many serious students who want to take lessons, which can be discouraging if you are trying to make a living. The task of keeping students and keeping them playing can be very difficult for instructors because they are competing with required academics and extra-curricular activities. Many find it difficult to practice or to play because they struggle with trying to keep up with all the demands on their time. This leads to frustration for the student, their parents, and their music instructor. In this highly competitive world in which we live, many activities entail an 'all or nothing' approach. If students are too exhausted to practice due to the sheer volume of demands on their time, usually music lessons are the first activities to be sacrificed. Many will quit playing the second their parents stop forcing them to take lessons. In some cases, however, students continue with lessons, after they discover that playing piano can be therapeutic and something that they will be able to enjoy for the rest of their lives.

The Simply Music method increases the likelihood of retaining students despite schedules because it is an easy way of learning to play the piano. It is fun. Students are experiencing 'hands-on' success and want to learn more. With the manageable pace of the method, many students feel that they can devote a small amount of time to daily practice. Even though they live busy lives, they can achieve their musical goals. They can find the time to practice most days at a fairly regular hour. A consistency will develop and practicing will then become a habit and not a chore. They develop responsibility for their progress and this ensures that they have the drive to keep studying the piano. This responsibility ties in directly to helping students become self-generative rather than simply being given information and repeating it. They can learn responsibility by taking it upon themselves to learn a given task even if it is not necessarily asked of them.

This method also allows instructors to work with students either individually or in groups. If an instructor works with groups, there is a greater potential for more income and less time devoted to working many hours. The instructor may choose what works better for them and their schedules. Some prefer to teach all group lessons, while others prefer to teach all private lessons, and still others prefer a mix of the two. Sometimes, the location of a studio, family commitments, studio size, schedule availability, or the economy, can affect how one handles their scheduling and the types of classes offered. Simply Music teachers have the freedom to choose.

What the Traditional Teacher Gives Up

As a professional musician steeped in the traditional way of teaching and learning music, I can understand many traditional teachers' reticence about the method. After all, would a traditionalist be selling out? Not really. There are many different philosophies to educating children so why should there not be different approaches to music education as well? Sometimes it is beneficial to try a new approach and expand our teaching philosophies. There are some things lost, however. Teachers give up four aspects of the traditional educational method when teaching the Simply Music method.

First, a Simply Music teacher gives up the freedom of deciding repertoire or what songs to teach. The Simply Music program is progressive. The repertoire is set up and planned out carefully to allow students to work and digest certain challenges one step at a time. Each idea tends to build on another. A song does not need to be learned all at once. Pieces can be broken down into small dosages to suit the needs of the student. Students do not usually realize that these foundational elements are occurring throughout the learning process. Once a piece is learned, it's expected to be maintained in good playing condition. Because the method is so completely thought out and tested, a Simply Music teacher need not work as hard to produce results. It is a very easy method to teach especially if an instructor has a musical background.

Second, if a teacher teaches in a group setting, the personal connection to students in some group settings can be less intimate. Sometimes this is a positive aspect to teaching the method because it allows more time for learning and less time for chatting and commiserating.

Third, a Simply Music teacher gives up fewer complaints and excuses for the teacher. With Simply Music it takes much less time and energy for students to experience results than with other methods. Typically, as a traditional student learns a new piece, it may take several weeks before that piece actually begins to sound like a song. All students must practice slowly, drill, repeat, etc. It can be a grueling and discouraging process. With Simply Music, the process is natural, seems painless, and is more rewarding.

Fourth, initially the teacher gives up page-based teaching style. The learning-through-doing makes perfect sense. We can read all of the books and manuals necessary to perform a certain task. But, until we are able to experience the task, it does not really make much sense. So often in traditional lessons, a student reads off the printed page. When a pianist is dependent on what is written on the page, musicality tends to whither away. I have seen this time and again and I, too, was one of those students. I became so consumed with what was on the written page that I forgot that I was supposed to be making music. Because I had been in that mode for so much of my young career, it was a struggle when I actually wanted to get away from the score and make music.

Also, a teacher who follows Simply Music recommendations can stop short-changing themselves. They are paid what they are worth. Teachers should be paid for a commitment of their time. This includes any makeup lessons resulting from the student's absence that so often impinge on the teacher's time. Simply Music also helps the music teacher to become an efficient and satisfied business owner. So much more goes into being a music instructor than just music lessons. Studio management and administrative duties are crucial to running a successful studio. The Simply Music method gives instructors the training and ability to manage their studios in a business-like fashion. There are so many business benefits gained by being a Simply Music teacher.

Finally, the effective Simply Music teacher transfers responsibility for the success of the students to the parents. The parents are accountable for assuming the work at home gets done. If the parents are not involved with their child's lesson and practice schedule, how can the child be expected to succeed? If parents are in lessons and are actively participating, they can then help the child at home during practice time. Maybe they, too, will learn to play the piano or learn a new technique of playing. The parents are ultimately held accountable for the success of their children.

The Business of Competing for Students

Now to the subject of competing with teachers for students: in this highly competitive profession, traditional teachers are always fighting for students. A teacher must always sell oneself in various ways in order to entice students to study with them. This can be truly frustrating for many professional musicians because they have had to jump through the hoops, pay the dues, pay for their education since the time they started lessons, and prove that they are worthy of being a legitimate teacher. Music school is exceedingly competitive and it either makes or breaks a student. Some students are more competitive than others. Teachers can sometimes be the deciding factor in whether a student at the upper echelons remains in music school. So after traditional teachers experience these trials, you would think that we are home free and that students should be knocking down our door wanting to study with us. But no, it does not happen that way. Sometimes, no amount of credentials will matter to people, only the right price. However, with Simply Music the competitive edge is diminished because the program sells itself. Simply Music teachers don't have to clamor for students. After the appropriate training, it's easy to share the message of Simply Music to others.

The Value of Teaching the Simply Music Way

So, all in all, is it worth it to learn to teach the Simply Music way? I believe that it has been very valuable to me and to my students. I have become a more knowledgeable and well-rounded teacher. I have met some wonderful instructors who are really doing a great job teaching this method and who are instilling the love of playing into their students versus beating it out of them. I believe that I am educating students in a nurturing and constructive way and that I am teaching them the value of self generation and responsibility. I am certain that I am educating parents as well in the value of supporting their children. It is not always easy to reiterate the concepts of responsibility into the parents' and students' minds, but in the end it pays off because the two parties will be much happier and satisfied. The responsibility of the parents and students will ensure the likelihood that students will maintain music as a lifelong companion. My business is thriving and I owe it all to the creation of this method.

§§§

I will never, ever, ever return to the traditional approach! The students I teach who want, deeply and truly, to express themselves musically – ARE! I can't tell you how profoundly Simply Music's approach to piano lessons, and to music, has changed my life.

Cindy Bettinger, Simply Music Teacher
Charleston, Illinois

CHAPTER 6

A TALE OF
THREE PIANOS

The Surprise Journey of a
Classically Trained Student

By Jacinta Kolomanski
Melbourne, Victoria, Australia

*Jacinta Kolomanski is a graduate of the University of Melbourne
in Law and Arts. She was admitted to practice as a barrister
and solicitor of the Supreme Court of Victoria in 1981. She also
obtained a Graduate Diploma in Education (Music) and for ten
years ran music programs catering to mothers and babies, and
pre-school children.*

The First Piano

My first memory of the piano occurred forty-nine years
ago. I was three and my mother was visiting a friend who lived
in an old, bluestone Victorian country house. The property
had once been a dairy and the yard was scattered with
outbuildings and sheds which were so common on Australian
farms of that vintage. This place was not in the country, rather
hidden along the Merri Creek, only four miles from the centre

of Melbourne. We entered through the kitchen, which was cool and dark. It must have been summer because I remember moving from the heat of the day into the hallway. It was vast, with many doors leading off to the left and right, big enough for a game of indoor cricket. The light streaming through the leadlight glass of the front door drew me on to the parlour, immediately to the right, and there in the corner was the piano.

It was a small cottage piano with a wooden frame. In its whole life, I doubt that it was ever in tune. Purchased with ration tickets during the Second World War, the harshness and aridity of Australian summers and the cold, damp Melbourne winters had twisted its frame so that the sound emanating was always short and cheerful, reminiscent of a music hall. As a three-year-old, I had found the most fantastic toy; I spent hours on subsequent visits trying out all the notes, pushing the pedals, and experimenting with sound. From the owner, I heard fantastic tales of parties where everyone would sing around the piano. More incredibly, I heard stories of my grandmother playing music for the dancing that seemed to be part of every social occasion. I was to witness that reverie only once. As a four-year-old, wrapped up in a dressing gown at a New Year's Eve party, I watched "grown ups" singing and dancing to the strains of <u>Auld Lang Syne</u>. Now, much later in life, when I practise this song, I am transported to a fabled era when the piano was the central part of the home and the conduit for happiness and joy.

The Second Piano

Some time later, my grandmother came to live with us bringing with her an iron framed upright piano. Her sadness was such that she never played and the piano languished in a corner jammed behind a large table. About the age of five, I was taken to see a revival of <u>The Wizard of Oz</u> at the cinema. In the early sixties, we were still a family without a television so an excursion to see a film was a source of great excitement. I was captivated by the song <u>Somewhere, Over the Rainbow</u>. My fascination was so great that the sheet music arrived home and thus began my forty-five year struggle with the piano. What did all those lines and dots mean? What were those funny squares above the lines with more dots? I had to know. I wanted to play that song on the piano and sing like Judy Garland. My persistence was rewarded by the promise that when I was seven, I could have lessons. My parents had sought advice from well meaning friends who believed in the Conservatorium model. No piano lessons until the child could read. The irony was that although I had taught myself to read before I went to school, the piano remained in the corner fenced in by other furniture for another two years.

Finally, in 1965, the piano was wrestled from its prison behind the cedar table and moved to a more prominent place in our home and I began piano lessons. At my first lesson, I was instructed to locate middle C, which I promptly fixed in my brain as the white key next to the latch. I was then given Book One of the <u>Leila Fletcher Piano Course</u>. I learnt that "music" was concealed on the page, but it could be decoded. It was very mysterious. I had to learn the secret clues to unlock and unravel the mystery. It was something that could only be revealed to those who had passed through complicated rites of initiation.

First, my eyes had to decode the symbols and then my hands would be directed to a place on the keyboard. My hands were merely the mechanical means by which those symbols would be translated into sound. Second, there was rhythm which was a strict arithmetical formula that had to be obeyed. The metronome swung tyrannically back and forwards to ensure that my fingers adhered to the tempo. Third, I discovered that music was not something that you enjoyed, but rather an exercise which would be examined on an annual basis. The half-remembered childhood promise of the joy, of friends singing around the piano, was soon abandoned in the terror of learning the required list pieces for the examination. The terror was heightened by the knowledge that you would get higher grades if you could play the pieces from memory. Being transfixed by the symbols on the page, I could never play without the security of the "music" in front of me. It never occurred to me that I was creating that music. In fact, when I played I never looked at my hands at all.

And so for forty weeks each year for the next ten years, I persevered with weekly lessons. The repertoire was strictly classical and whilst on my way through the grades, I learnt all the scales major, minor, both harmonic and melodic, and chromatic. My fingers swept along the keyboard with arpeggios and broken chords and they could play all the exercises in Hanon. However, I was alienated from *process*. The love of music was gone. I had not unlocked its mystery. Like schoolwork, it was merely something else to be measured and judged. The prospect of the weekly lesson would create such anxiety, that I would awake in the morning dreading the day to come. In the end, as final school exams loomed and with university around the corner, I took charge and decided to end the misery. My grandmother summed it up, "Pity you had all those lessons and you still can't sit down and play."

I became a lawyer. I married and had two beautiful daughters. In motherhood, that latent urge to find the music

65

resurfaced. I desperately wanted to give my girls the 'golden ticket' to that world which I had not entered. By the 1980's the value of music in early childhood was being flagged. I took my daughters to mother/baby music classes. It was a revelation. Here we were singing and dancing and having fun and there was music! So much fun that I had to know more. Not so much had changed after all from that five-year-old who wanted to sing like Judy Garland. I undertook further study – a post graduate diploma in music education. I reviewed all the available music methods – Kodaly, Orff, Dalcroze, Suzuki, and some commercially designed early childhood music programs. All had much to offer. I was entranced. I gave up law and ran a business for ten years running early childhood classes in community centres around Melbourne.

In the meantime, one of my brothers was making a name for himself in the commercial and academic music world. I was in awe of his talent. I was so proud of being related to a recognised composer, but at the same time jealous that he had found the key to the mystery which had eluded me. In my classes, I was facilitating a musical experience for others, but was not engaged in the creative process myself. At the end of the decade, my children were well established at school and I returned to law. My only connection with music was driving children to lessons and supervising practice times.

The Third Piano

With my youngest daughter enjoying her piano lessons and upon receiving a legacy, I decided to honour my grandmother's memory by buying a grand piano. With this magnificent instrument in its walnut case in our lounge room, my husband asked me to find him a piano teacher. I immediately knew that a traditional method would not suit him. Once again, I had to find out what else was available. Fortune smiled on my search and I found Kerry Hanley and Simply Music in the next suburb. We both attended Kerry's introductory talk. Unfortunately, my husband could not commit to the programme because of his work responsibilities. However, I was intrigued with the process that Kerry had described so, rather than my husband enrolling, I became the student instead. My grandmother's legacy was to trigger a profound change of direction in my musical education

At the outset, I made the decision to respond only to what was taught in the lesson. I put away my music books to make sure that I could not cheat. I wanted to be a complete beginner and to learn to approach music making in a new way. Obviously, as a person with previous piano experience, I was familiar with the landscape of the piano and fortunately had fingers that had maintained their dexterity. However, despite my perceived willingness to adopt a new way of learning, I conceitedly assumed that I would race through the levels. As I have discovered over the past three years, I had not envisaged the challenges that the Simply Music programme would throw up to me.

I have had to yield to the process and to resist my impatient urge to predict the next step. I have had to acknowledge new ways of learning and in doing so, put aside the intellectual arrogance that law school teaches and embrace a process which truly is an integration of mind, body, and soul. In that self-imposed struggle to accept a new way, I resisted and made life difficult for myself. Thankfully, I was not alone. Kerry was there to be my guide.

I have had to dismiss the memories of the 'Ghosts of Music Teachers past'. The punitive judgmental teachers of my youth have vanished. Kerry Hanley is not really my teacher at all, but rather my musical coach encouraging and urging me forward. At the outset, I did not know how my journey with Kerry would challenge me to examine ingrained attitudes; to open and examine emotional wounds and teach me to trust and believe in my own ability, and in that mix, allow me the freedom to play the piano. With her assistance, I have made a real discovery. Learning to play the piano with Simply Music is a journey and not an outcome.

Sometimes the way has been rocky and blocked by seemingly insurmountable obstacles. These obstacles are not of Simply Music's making, but all of my own design. Kerry gently prods me to keep going; counselling me and providing new strategies to overcome the impasse. She is gentle when I cannot seem to grasp the concept, but robust in her insistence that I proceed. For example, years of classical training shut me off from the rhythms of Jazz and Blues. The terror of aural musicianship exams left me petrified. Yet, despite my fear and anxiety, I am learning to embrace rhythmic dictation. The more I practise, the more I hear the patterns. I am becoming confident in my ability to learn and master new ideas despite my past experiences. This confidence spills over into everyday life.

Moreover, I have learnt efficient ways to practise. My memory has improved so that I learn new material faster. At the beginning, my anxiety was such that remembering the first phrase of <u>Dreams Come True</u> was exhausting. Now I watch my fingers on the keyboard. I notice their placement between the black and white keys. I pay attention to the groupings of black notes. It is akin to seeing something anew after years of apparent familiarity.

On the Simply Music journey there is always an exciting new vista. Presently, I am embarking on a new voyage. I am learning to "read". I am now enthusiastically putting aside what I already know and adopting a new way of looking at those symbols on the page. However, this time my hands are part of the process. In fact, it is becoming a total sensory experience. My middle-aged brain is creating new neural pathways as it integrates and coordinates all these new sensations. The key is the integration. I am saying, hearing, and doing on the physical level. But on an emotional level I am releasing old patterns of behaviour and learning new ways to respond and to attack new problems as they arise.

Simply Music has given me at mid-life a new way of looking at the world. The transformations have been two-fold. On one hand, the preconditioning of the past is being peeled away like the layers of an onion. As each layer is stripped away, my mind becomes less cluttered. I feel lighter and my thinking has more clarity. I recognise patterns and can remember songs in a more coherent manner. I no longer panic when a song is not at my fingertips. I just reflect on the technique Kerry has demonstrated and wait. I can sit at the piano for several hours at a time and play for my own enjoyment. Time seems to stop as I play.

On the other hand, the accompaniment program and the natural way Kerry has introduced me to composing my own songs has been liberating. Initially, I did not believe that I could compose. My brother is a *serious* composer. How could I dare to create a piece of music without years of study and a PhD? Yet, I have been given the freedom to create and compose without judgment. I have learnt that it is acceptable to make a mistake. What is even more invigorating is that composing is treated as a natural progression to playing and not as a dark art reserved only for the initiated. My compositions are simple and may not stand up to academic criticism, but I am relishing the pleasure that they give me. They are another step in the journey in a landscape which is constantly changing and increasingly becoming more exciting.

After three years as a student with Simply Music, what I know is this; I have embarked on a surprising journey. After a life time of antagonism, the piano is finally my friend – an instrument of infinite possibilities and a vehicle for life-long creativity. I am so grateful that I found the Simply Music programme. I am indebted to Kerry Hanley for her boundless patience and skilful guidance. Long may she teach and inspire others!

I have found the 'golden ticket'. Finally, music making is in my grasp. All I have to do is trust the process and let go. It's that simple.

§§§

I attempted to learn to play piano several times throughout my childhood and adult life. The results of traditional piano teaching methods were not stellar in my case. After years of stops and starts, I had a repertoire of only two songs and could only play if I had sheet music in front of me. Not until I found the Simply Music method did I ever feel I could really play piano. I now have a significant repertoire. I feel empowered to improvise and create music on my own. I entertain myself at the piano and play for an hour easily without ever looking at a sheet of music. Thank you, Simply Music!

Carrie Glicksteen, Student, Age: 58
Oak Park, California

CHAPTER 7

Defeating the Voice of "I Can't"

Overcoming the Impossible

By Stan Munson
Cleveland, Ohio

Stan Munson is a teacher who loves teaching. He graduated from California State University in Sacramento in Mathematics and is a credentialed teacher. In his spare time, he reads books on a wide variety of subjects that span technology, psychology, and theology. His most favorite thing to do is to hang out with his family and play the piano.

The Message

For most of my life, I've battled with an inner voice. It began in the third grade. I received a message that would be indelibly etched in my young, impressionable mind. Let me tell you what happened. One day, my teacher led us down to a room full of musical instruments. As the twenty or so kids arrived, there were others waiting. I was bug-eyed. Drums, horns, guitars, and flutes were among the many instruments there. We were encouraged to play around and explore the instruments. After about fifteen minutes, a group of us was led out of the classroom and the rest stayed behind. Now, Mrs. Greene never said it, but the message was clear, "You aren't musical." It probably didn't help that I picked up a flute and held it like a clarinet.

In fourth grade, a classmate played the piano in the cafeteria. It was in the middle of the room and chairs were set up around it. When he played, I was impressed and inspired. From that day on, I had an overwhelming desire to play the piano. Past thoughts crept into my mind; I wasn't musical or so I was told. I could play – but not the piano. Maybe, it wasn't for me.

A Patient Teacher

After seven years in the Coast Guard, I took a career placement test to see what I should do with the rest of my life. The computer kicked out three options. The only one that interested me was becoming teacher. But what kind of teacher? I love mathematics so I decided to complete a degree in Math.

Ironically, I had failed eighth grade math and had to attend summer school. That summer changed my attitude toward math. While there, I was fortunate enough to encounter a fabulous teacher. Mr. Gabinouski believed in me. He rebuilt my confidence and showed me the beauty in math. He told me, "You can do it." This teacher planted a seed in me that would grow into a love for mathematics. However, the most important thing that I learned from him was the profound effect of a patient teacher. He always took the extra time to teach me and encourage me.

While working on my degree, I needed general classes to create a well-rounded program. So I took a fine arts class called Beginner Piano. I thought, "Look, I am an adult now and I will decide if I am musical or not." Sadly, it was the only class I failed in college. I had two ways to view this. One, I was not meant to play the piano. Two, I didn't sell my soul to the devil like all piano players must have done. The message was solidified, "I am not musical". It was time to realize that the music world didn't include me – that people like me are just confined to listening and not participating. And so I moved on.

I got my degree in math and started my career teaching high school. I absolutely loved my job. As a teacher, I often reflect back on my experience with Mr. Gabinouski. I tried to be a patient teacher, to give special attention to students who believed the thoughts, "I can't do this."

The Calling

After teaching for eleven years, my family and I moved to Cleveland, Ohio to help plant a new church. My daughter started Simply Music piano lessons with Nancy LaJudice. As someone that longed to play the piano, I was impressed with the quality and quantity of music my daughter was playing in a short period.

One day, I had a free moment to attend my daughter's lesson along with my wife. Nancy casually mentioned, "Hey, if you know of anyone interested in being a piano teacher, have them call me." I was ending my one-year commitment with the church plant. I wanted to go back to teaching, but positions in my area were few and far between. When she said this, it was as if I had been kicked in the chest. I had an incredible feeling that these words were meant for me. But how could this be possible since "I am not musical". Certainly, I can't become a piano teacher. I can't learn how to play the piano this late in life, can I? No way would I ever jeopardize my family, my career of eleven years to start a new endeavor because of a dream that had been squelched so long ago.

For several weeks, I couldn't think of anything else. I struggled with the thoughts that plagued me from my past.

I contemplated what I would give up, how it would affect my family, my provision for them. I sought some needed advice. I talked in great lengths with Nancy and spoke with Neil Moore, founder of Simply Music, about my teaching experience and coaching skills. He asked me if I was coachable, that is teachable. He concluded that despite my inability to play, my background in coaching individuals/small group leaders and teaching gave me the tools needed to be a good teacher. After much thought and prayer, I took the plunge and decided to become a Simply Music teacher.

The decision was not an easy one. I was leaving behind a career that I loved. But I sensed a calling, a drawing to become a Simply Music teacher. I laid out the steps I thought were necessary to become a piano teacher. Here is what I consider the first and foremost step: learn piano!

I started telling my friends. Some were very encouraging and excited for me, but most thought I was nutty. A friend even asked, "Are you drunk?" In fairness to them, I am a little nutty, but it wasn't helpful hearing it from them. Funny, how those closest to us can discourage us the most. They didn't understand my deep-seated need to become musical.

I started piano lessons with Nancy. Throughout the process, I consistently heard this internal voice saying, 'I can't do this." Nancy taught me the first song, <u>Dreams Come True</u>. What a perfect beginning for me. Here I was, playing the piano. With both hands! I couldn't believe it. I can't possibly tell you how moved I was when I realized I was doing something I had thought impossible since elementary school. I continued to believe that sooner or later I would encounter a song that I could not play. When Nancy would demo each new song I would say, "Yup, that's the deal breaker."

Ten months after playing for the first time, just a few months after completing the Teacher Training Program, I opened Musical Bones Studio. I told everyone about this incredible non-traditional program. In my circle of friends, I had only one person sign up his kids for lessons. A part of me understands why. They knew me as this guy going into this unknown venture reserved only for the trained elite. I was an amateur, a novice, and I had only been playing piano for ten months. I am sure they thought, "How could Stan teach something he doesn't know." Our culture says only a classically trained pianist with years of experience can teach piano. I say with confidence, "Hogwash."

I once heard a story about Sherm Chavoor, swim coach for Mark Spitz and six other Olympic swimmers. Sherm was not an accomplished swimmer. One of his protégés remembers seeing Sherm get into the water only once. It was not his swimming skills, but his coaching skills that created Olympic swimmers. In my opinion, the best mentor is one that is just a few steps ahead of the student because the mentor then can easily relate to that student, as they reflect on their own recent journey. Overall, this has been my experience.

I am very open with potential clients. I tell people right off, "I am not the gem in this program. The gem is Simply Music. If you think you need a concert level pianist to reach your goals, this is probably not the studio for you. But if your goal is to be playing a large repertoire of songs in many genres, to have a personal relationship with the piano that includes improvising and composing, if you desire a coach that understands struggle and has patience with students' progress, then frankly, I don't know of a better program or coach."

This openness has dissuaded several prospective clients, but I think I make for a great testimony to what Simply Music accomplishes in a short period. It's not an accident that 60% of my students are adults. They relate to my story. They've always had this dream. They thought piano lessons were for kids. They thought it was too late. My story helps people see a dream come to reality. I am energized by that. It confirms my calling and passion.

Changing for the Better

As much as I liked teaching high school, it's much more fun teaching piano and running a studio. My studio is in my house; it's easy to go to work. Because of this, I appreciate the convenience and the physical closeness that I maintain with my family. I love the freedom of being self-employed. I'm also more confident as a leader; I own a piano studio and that takes some leadership skills.

Going through the Teacher Training Program has given me tools that I can use for the rest of my life. For example, the 'Long-Term Relationship' concept has helped me to manage relationships. Understanding the three realities of relationships, 'peaks, plateaus, and valleys', is very empowering for me as a husband, teacher, and friend. I am more intentional as a father. Piano lessons have provided my kids and I teachable moments and great conversations about how long-term relationships work. I warn them specifically that the valleys – the down moments – are temporary. When they started lessons, they 'pre-agreed' that they wouldn't quit in a valley. When the valleys come, I give them tools to navigate those tougher times. I know these conversations give them strength when they go through the times which are not much fun. My hope is that they will recall these conversations and apply these tools in their friendships, jobs, and marriages as they move through this world. Personally, I wish I had learned this sooner in life.

To Teach is to Touch Eternity

Teaching can be one of the noblest professions. It can have an everlasting impact on many people. Therefore, I took my high school teaching seriously. I, now, take my being a Simply Music teacher just as seriously. While student teaching back in college, I designed a poster of a hand (similar to Adam's hand, painted on the ceiling of the Sistine Chapel) touching a series of stick people who were also holding hands. Those stick people, getting smaller and smaller, appeared to form a spiral of people that descended infinitely into the center of the poster. The caption read To Teach is to Touch Eternity.

I realize that for some teaching piano is just a job. For me, this is more than a paycheck or a hobby. This is the beginning of a dream; a dream that doesn't stop with me. It's a privilege to help someone else accomplish their desires. I realized long ago that teaching in general has a real impact on someone's life. Most of my students come into my studio for the first time saying to themselves, "I can't do this." Continually, I make it my goal to help the student fight these thoughts. I know I am making a significant impact, changing the way a person thinks. Perhaps, their success in Simply Music will give them courage in other areas of their lives, pursuing passions that they never thought possible. I do know what impact Nancy LaJudice's decision to teach me has had on my life. And I am so thankful!

Support System

In January of 2010, I went to my first International Simply Music Symposium. I had only been teaching for about six months. To be honest, I was pretty scared to go. I thought I would be found out to be a fraud. I speculated there would be all these very talented people who had years of experience. I thought

77

once they heard me talk, or heard my story, or saw me play, they would say something like, "What the heck are you doing here?" This didn't happen. But what I encountered blew me away.

There was an array of teachers with various musical backgrounds and experiences. They had a deep passion for teaching others how to play the piano. These teachers didn't hold their skills over my head, but instead freely placed them into my hands. I must confess that I am such a "little girl" sometimes. I called my wife that first night and cried on the phone. I was so incredibly happy with the culture I was encountering, so overjoyed with the experience. I felt so accepted and supported; it was overwhelming. I have since discovered these teachers are a group of people bent on the mission of changing the music culture, tearing down walls that prevent people from experiencing their musicality. These teachers reach out to those who've said, "I can't do this," and change the world one student at a time. I identified with this because of my own personal journey. Through Simply Music, I've made some good friends around the world, particularly with the guys. It will be a lifetime of comraderie. I am so glad I went to the symposium. I left so energized and encouraged.

I realize I was walking a risky path when I chose to become a Simply Music teacher. I gave up financial security and resigned from the comfort of my career, which I enjoyed immensely, to follow a path I felt called to. The result is way beyond anything I had imagined. I am now part of one of the finest communities in the world, the Simply Music community. Not only am I playing the piano, but I'm teaching it. These people are not only my colleagues, but they are my friends/ mentors, committed to helping me become successful. That is satisfying and comforting all at once.

My Studio

I don't think I could ever have taught traditional lessons. The vast majority of those who take traditional piano lessons quit after their first or second year, never to return. Those people go on for the rest of their lives believing the internal voice that says, "I can't do this, I am not musical". As part of the Simply Music community, I am a teacher who combats this voice. I promote a different kind of narrative.

After a year of teaching, I have a studio of about twenty students. Running the risk of offending my colleagues, I confess that I have the best Simply Music students of any studio!

My very first student, Mason, was a five-year old, blind boy. He has a degenerative disease, Battens Disease, which leads to dementia and death in the early teens. His mother wanted to help her son experience his musicality before the inevitable door of opportunity closes for him. She told me that she called at least a dozen other music teachers and left messages with them. Others said that they had nothing for him since he was blind. Some didn't take the time to call her back. But I knew with Simply Music that I had a lot to offer him. I understood his mother's deep desires as well. So, without reluctance, I took him on as a student. Mason has struggled with learning piano. I am convinced his struggle was more a function of his 'fiveness' than his blindness. What I mean is that many kids his age struggle with coordination and identification of their digits; so did he. He was on the young side of starting lessons and those struggles were compounded by his blindness. Doctors and others who mean well, remind his mother that, "yesterday was his best day." In piano, this hasn't been the case. This year, he has shown great progress. He took about a year to learn the first song, <u>Dreams</u>. Now, that is tenacity! And the second song, <u>Storm</u> is coming even quicker. His mother says his doctors are amazed that he is learning to play. He thinks I am teaching him piano, but the reality is that he is teaching me about life. How cool is that?

Stephen, an adult student of mine, had four years of 'traditional' lessons at a prestigious music school. The level of music attained during those years wasn't much and looking at sheet music still gives him great anxiety. He talks about how he had to play from a child-like songbook and all the songs were about some pony. After the third song, all he wanted to do was kill the pony! Without a doubt, he can say that Simply Music far exceeds his first program in the quality of music, quantity of music, and the feeling of accomplishment. Now, he regularly plays in public places without the music in front of him. The joy of playing has been restored. This is a complete stretch from his prior experience.

Then there is the seventy-five-year-old grandmother, Adeline, who grew up in a musical family. She has memories of her family around the piano; her mother playing the piano, her dad playing the accordion, and all the siblings singing together. As a grandmother, she realized she had not passed that gift on to her own children. So she decided to take up piano lessons to create those memories for her grandchildren. I told her it wasn't too late to start and she became my Simply Music student.

I wanted to create those same kinds of memories for my family. I absolutely love the mini-concerts we have in the 'Elmbrook Room at Munson Hall' (our home). My kids and wife are also learning to play. Some nights, we all gather around the piano and play songs and sing. I am confident that incredible memories are being formed that will last a lifetime.

80

It is such a gift! These memories never would have happened if Simply Music had not entered my life.

Simply Music has made an incredible impact on me. It has been no small affair. The voice that once haunted me is slowly fading away into the background of piano music. The words, "I can't do it," has shifted to, "Yes, I can." I am winning this challenge. And living out my passion. Not only that, this calling provides the opportunity to affect others in such a profound way for the rest of their lives. It is such an honor to be a part of people's stories. What a fulfilling and satisfying life! Though I considered it once impossible to play the piano, I see now that I *can* do it. I am a Simply Music teacher. I *am* musical.

§§§

I am a Simply Music teacher who had my first piano lesson six months before I started teaching it. I teach more than fifty students of various musical backgrounds each week, many of whom are adults, and some in their 60's and 70's. There is no question in my mind that of all the things that I have learned as an adult, piano has been the most meaningful and profoundly fulfilling element added to my life.

Kelly Carter, Simply Music Teacher
Markham, Ontario, Canada

CHAPTER 8

A GRANPARENT'S WISDOM

Sharing the Joy of Music

By Randy and Peggy Skinner
Greenwood, South Carolina

Randy and Peggy Skinner are proud grandparents to five grandchildren, of which Kara Skinner is the youngest. They believe that music is so important for children, especially in the first six or seven years of a person's life! They are impressed with the way Simply Music is helping Kara with all of her academic progress, especially learning to read and write, and seeing patterns in math.

Playing Immediately

Kara Skinner just turned seven. She takes piano at our hometown. In reality, her story 'doesn't qualify' – she has had seven lessons in six months. We live in different states and have to work around holidays, birthday parties, and all the usual family considerations. Kara visits us every two to three weekends and takes a piano lesson each time she visits. The only opportunity she has to practice is when she visits us. Kara has found the joy of music and of playing the piano through the Simply Music method.

What makes her learning process unique is that she can already play the first two songs in the Simply Music program perfectly! Her improvisation is played in such a lively, entertaining manner that this pair of grandparents don't want to miss a beat. We are amazed at how quickly her efforts produce beautiful music.

We have found that music adds to a child's happiness. Stirring the senses, of course, but it also provides a reason to set personal goals, such as being able to sing a song and take pride in sitting at a piano knowing you've accomplished a new challenge.

We gladly purchased a keyboard at the time of her first lesson. At present, Kara doesn't have the luxury to play and practice at her home. A couple of weeks pass with no practice. We hurry in on a Friday evening after the drive from Georgia, squeeze in practice, and then she can hardly wait to play for Ms. Susan Justesen on Saturday morning. After class, she is anxious to show Granddaddy her next goal.

Seeing a child's face light from within as she discovers her own ability warms our hearts. It adds so much to her self esteem. Kara has only just begun a love of music that will grow as she grows. This clever style of teaching piano stimulates the learner and opens the door to individual creativity. Our gift of lessons is a gift returned in the richest manner!

§§§

In our family, music was always an important part of our children's education. We are happy as grandparents that we made the decision to support our granddaughter in Simply Music piano lessons. Our grandchildren are an extension of us. What an opportunity to be a part of developing their gifts, knowing we played a small part in their learning.

David and Sara Derksen, Grandparents
Didsbury, Alberta, Canada

CHAPTER 9

THE HEALING TOUCH

Personal Empowerment for a Blind Teacher

By Dodie Brueggeman
College Place, Washington

Dodie Brueggeman is Simply Music's first blind teacher. At the age of twenty, she lost her vision because of diabetes and spent the intervening years struggling for survival, reclaiming health and raising a daughter as a single mom. She appeared on Good Morning America *after riding a tandem bicycle across the United States with her husband.*

A Little History

As a blind adult, it took me fifty-three years to finally discover my perfect career. How did I ever achieve this absolutely satisfying experience? Days filled with purpose, a fulfilling career beyond anything I ever dreamed, a sharing of a gift that I only experienced myself for a brief time before it became the means of my financial security. When Simply Music entered my life, it more than met my needs and desires.

At age eight following a severe illness, I was diagnosed with diabetes; thus began my journey of many health problems. As a young newlywed, I lost my vision as well as my kidney health. During this difficult time, learning how to use a white cane was exciting. More challenges came my way. Not knowing that it typically takes a year or two to learn how to read and write Braille, I learned it in six weeks. Dialysis was not as readily available as it is today, so I tried an alternative approach that somehow managed to jumpstart my kidneys. My focus for the next twenty-seven years became one of rebuilding my health and regaining my kidney function. One added joy in my life, in the midst of my trials, was the adoption of my daughter. She brought fulfillment and delight to my days. Eventually, I finally received news of my first normal kidney function test. I was so thankful. But unavoidably, I was divorced in 2004.

Growing up, I had a few years of piano, but those years felt like nothing when I tried to play the piano after losing my vision. "This is as good as it will get," I told myself as I struggled to piece together favorite songs whenever I was around a piano. I had little access to a piano for many years until I bought one so that my daughter could grow up with an instrument in our home. My daughter had little interest and I didn't do much either, believing that my ability just wasn't enough to help me learn to play comfortably and joyfully.

A Financial Need

Just a few years ago, I was on a quest for employment to supplement my disability income. Options for a blind individual without a college degree didn't seem to exist. As a client of the Department of Services for the Blind (DSB), I began to explore work options. With their help, I planned to launch my education further in order to become qualified to work as a Teacher's Assistant in the Public School system. This idea was more an act of desperation than desire. I knew I needed to establish a source of supplemental income for the years ahead. Having spent a number of years doing volunteer work, I discovered that having to go out to a job day after day come rain or shine, sleet, snow or hail, took a toll on my health. I was also calculating how I would juggle an hour long bus ride each way between college classes and work in order to be home by 3:30 each afternoon for my school-aged daughter. "This is not really what I want to do, but what I need to do," I told myself. I was due to start college classes when my sister, Dixie Cramer, a Simply Music Teacher in training, encouraged me to look into Simply Music.

"I think you can do it. Why don't you check out the Simply Music website and then call Neil Moore, the creator of Simply Music, and see what he says. You know that his experience teaching a blind boy to play the piano is how Simply Music began." "I'll check it out," I told her as she departed... and I did. The website was fascinating! The statement Wade's father made about being pleased with his progress, causing Moore to completely redefine who could learn to play and who could learn to teach seemed to apply directly to me. By the next day, I was on the phone with Neil Moore. "I'm blind," I told him. "Can I do this?" He didn't tell me I could do it...instead, he had me telling him that I was sure I could do it. Determined to be a stay-at-home mom, I pursued this option.

A New Endeavor

I had three days to submit my application to Simply

Music to meet the teacher training cost deadline. I contacted DSB about help, but they were quite distressed with my sudden change of career direction. I knew Simply Music was the right choice for me. Not only would I be sharing a wonderful gift with others, but my need for supplemental income from a home-based business would be met. DSB believed it was too big a risk and they could in no wise meet the deadline. They indicated that it would be highly unlikely for them to support me in achieving employment status with Simply Music because they didn't see Simply Music as a viable option for a blind person's successful employment. With time pressing, I decided to leap out in faith on my own and succeeded in submitting my application and payment just under the deadline.

I began my training. Neil was very encouraging and we decided that a simple step-by-step process of the Teacher Training Program would eventually reveal just how far I could go. We left the outcome completely open-ended. I obtained a low interest loan and purchased a new faster computer as well as adaptive software which enabled necessary access to the teacher training materials. The training was long and tedious, but the fun came when I was able to listen to the training videos. It was easy to understand how a blind child could learn to play with the Simply Music method.

Finally, I became the world's first blind Simply Music teacher! At about the same time, another Simply Music teacher, Susan Jamison, moved to my town and contacted me. We came together often to polish our skills, support one another, and prepare to teach. We set our goal to begin in the coming year. We invited everybody we could and had a shared Free Introductory Session (FIS) – a presentation explaining Simply Music to prospective students.

With a studio of eight new students, I began teaching on January 8, 2006. I decided to specialize in working with adults. Susan was an incredible blessing to my advancement. She wrote descriptions of the reference books, wrote the lyrics and chords for the accompaniment program, and even tried helping me to tactilely mark the reference books with Braille and puff pens. Her energy, creativity, endurance, and loyalty abounded and we came to depend on each other as we grew our studios. Dixie, Susan, and I came together periodically to discuss strategies and encourage one another. With unflagging support from the Simply Music staff and teachers, my ability grew.

I dedicated hours each day to studying and learning the Simply Music way of learning and teaching. Some of my students were quite advanced at the onset and I struggled to stay ahead of them. Transferring some of my students to Susan or Dixie would not be possible because they quickly fell behind the first foundation levels I seemed to have rushed through. By this time, I was feeling overwhelmed and had moments of discouragement. My more advanced students had no desire to quit or transfer anyway and they urged me to study and see just how far I could travel with them through the Simply Music journey.

As I learned to play, I struggled with my memory. I had taken three students through the more advanced part of Simply Music, but it seemed quite a struggle for me to retain all the information thoroughly as I tried to memorize everything, including the specialized programs in Simply Music. Nevertheless, when I practice my entire playlist (repertoire of songs), I can play for over three hours! I am amazed at what I have been able to retain through the Simply Music way of learning.

DSB Assistance

After teaching for a year, I contacted DSB and asked them to assist me with job retention. I began to prepare myself for the reading part of Simply Music. I knew that I would have to learn how to read Braille Music Notation if I wanted to teach the reading part of Simply Music. After my first year of teaching, I submitted a copy of my tax return to DSB. They determined that my Simply Music career was 'gainful employment' and accepted me as a client once again. It was extremely gratifying to show that I had made a success of this incredible business opportunity.

After noting my obvious success, DSB purchased several very expensive items for me. The first was a software package called Dancing Dots. This package allows one to scan and edit print music and then convert it to Braille Music Notation. They also purchased computer screen reading software called JAWS (Job Access with Speech). The third item was a note taker called a PacMate which has a forty cell Braille display. The PacMate is vital as it enables me to read the Braille music files. I was so overwhelmed with the incredible learning curve for all of these items that I wondered at times if I would survive.

DSB also purchased hours of tutoring for the Braille Music reading process for me. My tutor, Dave Simpson, is a professional organist and singer who is blind. He has been a marvelous and valuable support. Eventually, with his tutelage, I learned my first song from Braille Music Notation. I still have quite a way to go as Braille Music is an incredibly involved and complex language. Besides learning to read what is called a bar over bar style, I am learning the paragraph style of music. A single measure for one hand can easily use thirty plus Braille characters.

Serving the Community

It gives me great satisfaction to know that somehow I've contributed to the greater good of the blind. As my relationship with DSB draws to a close, some of their counselors have called to inquire about Simply Music on behalf of other blind individuals who are seeking job opportunities. Also, while converting all of Simply Music's files into Braille Music Notation, I began to realize the unlikelihood of other individuals having the time and endurance to make these materials accessible. The work was tedious and took more of my time than most people would want to spend. It seemed ludicrous to envision others going through hundreds of hours of work to be able to have these materials at their fingertips. I thought, "Why should others have to re-create the wheel?"

I recalled that the Father Palmer Braille Service, a non-profit organization in my state, works to make textbooks accessible for elementary through college students. With their cooperation, we brailled all of the lyrics, numbers, and directions for the first four Simply Music Reference Books. Now, these reference books will be available to blind teachers, blind students, and their families. I am so excited by what has been accomplished already that I find myself highly motivated to complete the entire process for all the levels in Simply Music. With more work ahead of me, I revel in the knowledge that future blind teachers will struggle less in their learning process and sighted teachers will have far more to offer blind students.

Passing the Dream

I have absolutely no regrets concerning my choice to pursue Simply Music! I have much work ahead. It is comforting to embrace Neil Moore's quote, "It is a process, not an event."

When I look back five years to the beginning of my training, I am amazed at how far Simply Music has brought me! I have learned so much. It is an ongoing source of psychological, emotional, and spiritual fulfillment! The results of all the hard work are and will continue to be immensely satisfying.

Yes, a blind child opened the door for the development of Simply Music. That simple yet profound event has trickled down to the lives of thousands of individuals. I count myself blessed beyond measure to be among the hundreds of Simply Music teachers! In holding the distinction of being the first blind Simply Music teacher in the world, it is my hope that by pursuing my dreams more doors will open for others. No matter what difficulties they may face, they will be empowered and encouraged to reach out and achieve their own dreams.

§§§

My son has been learning with the Simply Music method for two years now and loves it. He was born with two fingers webbed together. He had surgery to repair it, but had been teased just enough to make him self-conscious about it. He is very intelligent, but introverted. He needed a voice, a way to express himself in a positive way. I heard about Simply Music through a friend and it sounded like just the thing he needed. The program is so smart. He could use his hands to create such beautiful music almost instantly! Suddenly his little imperfection turned into a gift.

Darlene Dominguez, Parent
Simi Valley, California

CHAPTER 10

MUSICAL
SELF-EXPRESSION

A Parent's Perspective on Learning and Creativity

By Pele Myers
Campbell, California

Pele Myers is a writer and graphic designer. Her son, Wade, started with Simply Music piano lessons when he was six-years-old. Eight years later, as a young man his journey with Simply Music continues.

The Challenge

Wade is a precocious, intelligent, independent child peppered with a strong will, creative imagination, and fearlessness. Typically, for a person with these qualities, *the world could be your oyster*. However, Wade has some challenges, obstacles to overcome. In short, he is a highly *sensory* child. Cumulative tests conducted when he was four to nine, concluded that he has an overly sensitive nervous system which manifests outwardly as oversensitivity to the environment and auditory processing disorder. He was not equipped with the normal auditory filtering system that most people have. When we went to Disneyland a few years ago, after one hour of people, rides, and sounds, he begged us to leave and return to the hotel room. When we attended family events with my large Italian family, within an hour of our visit, his eyes would glaze over and I could tell he had reached "overwhelm" and was mentally checked out. When we returned home, he shut himself up in his room and did imaginary play with *sound effects* as a way to decompress from the noise over-stimulation. In a classroom situation, Wade would hear every sound amplified, children talking, people moving around, papers shuffling, chalk moving on the chalkboard, pencils being sharpened, etc. The pencil sharpening noise was particularly painful to him. As a result, his focus at school was inconsistent.

In first grade, Wade learned concepts easily and had an inquisitive mind; however, as the day progressed and his nervous system fatigued more and more from auditory overload, he found the seatwork repetitive, boring and pointless, and would mentally check out or cause disruption in the classroom. Despite the teacher's efforts to coax, threaten, or discipline him for not completing seat work, he was stubborn and fearless. Once he decided he was done with everything he felt he should have to do, he was unbending and unafraid of the consequences that his teachers doled out. Of course, this led to many calls from the teacher or principal who didn't really understand him and thought that he was just being a troublemaker. So Wade felt that he was not being successful at school even though he learned things easily.

When he entered second grade, Wade couldn't focus or stay interested in school which now required more hours of seat work. He became impulsive, defiant, and easily frustrated. It was recommended that he return to first grade to give him more time to "mature" and to better handle the seat work demands. I knew these challenges were the result of the auditory sensitivity. Wade needed help! Wade is smart, but with these obstacles, it was quite difficult to channel his learning capabilities. We didn't realize it then, but Wade's help was already in progress.

The Answer

Earlier, I had read about programs where music was used to help children with auditory challenges. I thought that learning to play an instrument would be a good creative outlet for Wade. I had asked the music teacher at school if I could start piano lessons with him and she said, "No, it is too early. Wade's attention span is too short." She suggested waiting a few years. Wade was five-years-old at the time. My intuition told me that what the music teacher said was probably true for traditional piano lessons where there is a lot of focus on scales and reading and that this rote kind of learning would not interest or engage him. In essence, this method would have led to failure for a kid like Wade. So I began to seek non-traditional options. Within a few months, my sister told me that her daughter was learning piano using a method called Simply Music. As soon as she said the name, I got that tingle down my spine; you know, the tingle you get when your intuition tells you an important truth. Anyway, I immediately got the contact information and set up lessons.

Simply Music was the perfect way to learn to play the piano for a person like Wade. It allowed him to learn music using systems and memorization so he could immediately enjoy the success of playing songs without being bogged down with rote practice or trying to read and play at the same time. Since his attention span was quite short, his Simply Music teacher, Bernadette Ashby, focused on simple songs or small segments of songs at first so that he could experience a sense of accomplishment at each lesson. She was very patient with him and worked on keeping him focused with his limited attention span. She also challenged him to continuously stretch this span. Did Wade resist this stretching? Absolutely! Did he get distracted before the lesson was over? Yes, at first. Week after week, month after month, she held him accountable for practice of the entire playlist that he had learned and increased the complexity of the music segments, all the while encouraging him and explaining how each song was exercising and building his 'memory muscle'. This method was inviting to Wade because he felt successful each week.

As his attention span grew, his teacher gave Wade larger and more complex segments of songs to learn. He easily learned them and before long he had a repertoire of twenty songs; then thirty, then forty, etc. It wasn't until he had a firm grasp of the music from the first few Simply Music books that Mrs. Ashby introduced music reading. Since she had already introduced much of the music language and concepts (i.e. the names of chords, strong sense of rhythm, relationship between notes), the transition to music reading seemed natural and unintimidating. Wade loved the challenge of the more difficult songs and began to see how the strength of his memory was helping him with school work.

Fortunately, Wade's attention span improved at the piano; it also improved at school work. He was able to do longer sessions of seat work without distraction. His ability to memorize details in preparation for tests increased significantly. We noticed that he began to improve his math, science, and writing skills. At the end of second grade, Wade's school work and intellectual capability had improved so much that his second grade teacher and principal recommended that he skip third grade and go right into fourth grade. Wade's confidence increased as his academic performance improved.

Creative Freedom

His piano playing improved and by sixth grade he had not only a repertoire of at least one hundred songs, but he composed his own piece, <u>Parting of the Ways</u>, and played it for a recital and talent show. When Wade played this first composed piece at a talent show for his school in front of his peers, he sat at the piano and played with fearlessness, confidence, and a certainty. For this eleven-year-old, he had no doubt that he was displaying his true essential self at the piano. Afterwards, even the older students at his school came up to Wade and said, "That was cool!"

The more Mrs. Ashby challenged Wade, the more he challenged himself. For example, he would learn the traditional right and left-handed parts of a song and then he would cross him arms and play the song again using his left hand to play the right hand part and the right hand to play the left hand part. Also, he began to play some songs with his eyes closed. And finally, he would take some of the songs and improvise with different chords or add melodious segments in strategic places of the score. He was not afraid to try new things and Mrs. Ashby always encouraged his self-expression. If he was forced to learn or play music by rote until he played each song perfectly, he would quickly get bored. For a strong-willed and independent child like Wade, rearranging musical scores and trying new things was paramount for feeling successful and staying engaged. In other words, he started to appreciate that he had developed enough musical knowledge and skill to make the music his own. He was having fun with it!

Mrs. Ashby encourages Wade to find songs that he wants to learn so she can add them to the lesson time and his repertoire. Additionally, Wade has developed a love of many different types of music: Jazz, Classical, Rock, etc. He listens to music by a variety of artists and often will try to play some new songs on the piano from auditory memory of what he's heard. This exploration lends itself to continuing to develop his own compositions and enjoy the freedom of his own creativity.

For the first few years that Wade was learning to play piano, he used an electronic keyboard. We physically did not have room in our house for a piano. As we saw that music was continuing to be a positive part of his development and creative expression, we decided to remodel our house to make room for a *real* piano. A remodel meant tearing down a wall to open up the kitchen-living room area and make it one large room. So after almost two years of construction and disruption to our household, we completed the remodel and purchased a grand piano. He felt very blessed to begin playing on a *real* piano with keys, strings, and a foot pedal. He began to develop the finger strength which was lacking and unnecessary on an electronic keyboard. The finger strength along with the use of a real foot pedal improved the rhythm and musicality of his songs because the piano strings were able to resonate as intended to bring the music alive. It made him feel special to see his music come alive in a new way. When we have family or friends over, he will often bless them by playing a few songs. We told him that if he continues to play the piano, this piano will be his for his own home.

Wade is now thirteen-years-old and is still a highly sensory child. His nervous and auditory systems can still get overwhelmed, but playing the piano or listening to music is his favorite way to decompress and calm his nervous system. For a highly sensory child like Wade, providing structure and limiting unnecessary stimulation allows him to better manage his world. He maintains a consistent routine and structure. He does his homework as soon as he comes home from school and practices piano right after dinner. He maintains a playlist to track which songs he plays every day and ensure that he gets to all of them on a weekly basis. We notice that he often uses his quiet time to do imaginative play in his room, or draw, write stories, or *play around* on the piano, composing his own music.

Yes, Wade is a precocious, intelligent, independent child peppered with a strong will, creative imagination, and fearlessness – but playing music using the Simply Music method has channeled each of these characteristics in a positive way. Developing his memory, playing cross handed, and playing with his eyes closed have all helped to strengthen and organize his left and right brain performance. I believe these have promoted and engaged more of his intellectual potential at school, as evident by his vastly improved focus, ability to learn, and scholastic performance. He can do long stretches of homework without getting distracted and he does well on tests because he can retain lots of detail. He is able to negotiate better in noisy environments. Playing and listening to music has given him something positive and healthy to focus on so that he can de-focus from the noisy and over-stimulating world. Simply Music gives Wade a great tool to challenge and channel his strong will and creative imagination through learning new songs, creating his own variations of those songs, and crafting his own compositions. Wade has been blessed to see just a glimpse of how *the world could be his oyster*.

§§§

It has been amazing for me to watch our three sons learn to play the piano so quickly. Not only do children learn to play quickly with Simply Music, they feel so free and competent to explore music that they compose their own songs. Our nine-year-old and our twelve-year-old have both composed original songs. Music fills our house and our boys' hearts and I love that! Simply Music has been a gift for our family.

Duane Carlisle, Parent, Head Strength and Conditioning Coach
San Francisco Forty-Niners
Santa Clara, California

CHAPTER 11

GIFTS GIVEN TO ME

Playing in the Real World

By Adam King
Redding, California

Starting as a child, Adam King took lessons for many years from the founder of Simply Music, Neil Moore. He is using his God-given talents for the piano in many settings. Currently, he is the Youth Music Director at a local church. Adam has a passion for the piano and for music in general. He loves teaching children, teens, and adults alike.

The Gift

I've received a gift that I am so happy to give away. Not many gifts can make that claim, but the gift of music can. The piano is more than just eighty-eight keys of black and white. It goes much deeper than the thousands of moving parts below the polished wood. If no one is present to listen to your music, you can always play the melodies that are innate within your own soul. The piano also speaks as a medium, from the musician to all that have an ear. Through piano playing, I have met a Grammy-award-winning singer, I have played in front of thousands of people, as well as at more intimate dinner parties, and I have even romanced my wife through the piano's enthralling influence. Which door will this instrument open next? The possibilities are endless. You never know what conversations it will spawn and with whom. Music is a universal enjoyment. The piano being played in this way speaks more powerfully than any other instrument.

Simply Music has given me this gift. The journey started when I was eight-years-old and I had a burning desire to learn how to play the piano. My parents encouraged this desire and began the search for a teacher. Soon after, my dad was looking in the paper and saw an advertisement about a new piano-learning method from Australia. My parents and I attended a free information session with Neil Moore and decided to give this new method a try.

Neil Moore, the teacher, and I began a lasting relationship that was to change my life forever. I have so many childhood memories of my weekly lessons at his studio in downtown Sacramento. I remember thinking that the staircase to his studio was so long when I hadn't practiced enough, but I always left the lesson with a smile on my face and determination in my step.

My parents created experiences for me that always helped me to look forward to lessons. We made a tradition out of going to the nearby Chevron station and picking out an item of choice each week after lessons. Although this tradition was not good on our teeth, it was a small ingredient that made lessons a fun thing in my mind, helping to fuel my desire to become as good on the piano as I could be. I sometimes felt inferior to some of my peers, but as my new-found talent progressed I became known among them for my musical abilities. This speedy progression soon built up my self esteem and confidence.

Giving It Away

When I was eleven-years-old, my family helped initiate and lead a branch ministry of The Rock Church in a suburb of Sacramento. When the branch church began to thrive and had reached about sixty people in regular attendance, our music minister packed up his family and moved out of state. Because of the high standard of excellence he had brought to the music department, his vacancy left a huge hole in our Sunday services. With no one else to turn to, the pastor asked me to take the previous minister's place at the piano. I was extremely nervous and had only one church song in my repertoire.

I remember going to lessons that week and asking my teacher about my situation. I asked him if he could teach me how to play accompaniments on the piano. He paused and confidently gave a suggestion, "How about Amazing Grace?" He quickly figured out this accompaniment piece and taught it to me on the spot! From then on, we started learning accompaniments along with the other Simply Music material. Amazing Grace is now one of the first songs that Simply Music students learn in their Level I repertoire. For a short while, I could only play one accompaniment song, but as the weeks went by, much to the congregation's relief, we were able to put together quite a playlist.

I continued to play the piano every Sunday with the band at the branch church and also attended The Rock Church for night services on Sundays. Every year, The Rock Church put together a very large children's Christmas play. When I was twelve-years-old, the director asked me to perform a piece on the piano to open the play. One could imagine my trepidation at the idea of playing in front of over a thousand people. After overcoming the fear of playing in front of the branch church every week, my parents encouraged me to give it a shot. After many months of practice, my diligent work paid off. I remember working with my teacher for weeks to perfect the chosen piece for the play. This was one of the major milestones in my journey of learning to play the piano. Each small victory set me up to conquer the next challenge.

Discipline To Be Great

Even with my success on the piano, I went through periods that I lost almost all desire to keep practicing and, on a few occasions, even asked if I could quit. This goes to show how nearsighted young people can be when looking into the future. Wisely, my parents insisted that I continue to play because of the immense blessing that the piano had already been in my short life. I had built an identity for myself on the piano that I couldn't let go of. I continued to play through the years even after Neil was obligated to discontinue our private lessons in order to focus all of his attention on administratively building Simply Music as an international institution.

I went on to take many music theory classes at the local college and continued my music education. Over the years, I have been the music minister for five different churches. I also had the awesome experience of being able to travel the United States to play for various churches and events. I was privileged to play at a large church in New York City for a Grammy award-winning singer, Donny McClurkin. I am currently the music minister at a local church in northern California. I use the Simply Music method to work on accompaniments with band members and even vocalists. I also teach and run a large studio with Simply Music students of all ages.

I have come to realize that the one character trait that is required to be an accomplished musician is discipline. This one attribute separates "good" from "great" and is the ultimate bridge to success. Students who exhibit the greatest advances and success aren't necessarily the most talented or gifted. Students that take off like rockets are the ones that can do exactly what the teacher says and do it with all their might. If students are able to dedicate themselves to the method, it is only a matter of time before greatness is achieved. As one of the few who started taking lessons during the birth of Simply Music, I have been able to observe and experience the success of Simply Music first hand. I can say from my own testimony and from the observation of other students, that this method, when applied diligently, delivers success to both the student and the teacher. Having the ability to play such a magnificent instrument is truly a gift beyond compare.

§§§

During my time with the Simply Music program, I have furthered my knowledge on how to read sheet music and many other things. And now that I am in the worship team at my local church, I can put that knowledge to good use, praising and worshiping the Lord. I am anxious to continue my learning with Simply Music and the worship team.

Nathan Smith, Student, Age: 14
Stanhope, Iowa

CHAPTER 12

MY SPECIAL CHILD

A Parent's Thoughts on Autism and Piano Playing

By Deanna Pierre
Omaha, Nebraska

Deanna Pierre is a trained Industrial Engineer and also received an MBA from the University of Nebraska. She chooses to be a stay-at-home mother of five children. Her daughter, Celeste, was diagnosed with autism at the age of two. Contrary to any learning challenges, Celeste is excelling in her piano playing and sharing her gifts with others. Celeste is now sixteen-years-old.

The News

Celeste was diagnosed with "Pervasive Development Disorder-Not Otherwise Specified" (PDD-NOS) which is a neurological disorder on the autism spectrum. According to the Autism Society of America, "Autism is a complex developmental disability that typically appears during the first three years of life and affects a person's ability to communicate and interact with others. Autism is defined by a certain set of behaviors and is a 'spectrum disorder' that affects individuals differently and to varying degrees. There is no known single cause for autism." People with autism have a normal appearance, but often spend their time performing activities which are difficult to understand.

In Celeste's case, diagnosis was made at age two. She spoke no more than eight words at that time, made little eye contact, and had little interest in peer interaction or make-believe play. Any parent whose child has been given the diagnosis of autism typically goes through a period of grieving. They have to adjust their thoughts about their expectations and hopes for the life and the potential outcome of that child. We were no different. It took time for us to come to terms with having a daughter with special needs when we thought she would be perfect! By the grace of God, we have come to understand that all of us are imperfect; it is simply that some people's imperfections are easier to see than others. Celeste is not defective or lacking; rather, she is a child of God, created in His image and likeness, as we all are. She has her own gifts and talents, as each of us does. Every day we are reminded by Celeste's presence in our lives that it is not what you know or what you can do that is most important; it is that you ARE. Life is a precious gift from God and Celeste reminds us of this every day.

When Celeste was about nine-years-old, we were stationed at Hill Air Force Base in Layton, Utah, and I sought out a piano teacher for my children. The teacher I found taught the Suzuki method which I had heard about and was very interested in trying. I asked the teacher if she would be willing to try to teach Celeste. She agreed. However, at the end of the first lesson, she said that she could not teach Celeste because Celeste was not responsive enough. The teacher had no experience teaching autistic children to play piano and was apparently unable and unwilling to adapt her instruction to someone who *looked* as if she was not paying much attention. So lessons ended at that point for Celeste. I did not try to find another teacher at that time because I was waiting to see how my other children took to piano instruction with that particular method. They did well, but after one and one-half years, we moved to Nebraska and thus I was on a quest for a new teacher. I planned to find a Suzuki teacher, but, happily, Simply Music found us instead. Celeste is the second of our five children; three others are also currently in various levels of Simply Music instruction.

Finding the Right Method

Our introduction to Simply Music occurred in the most unlikely of places – in the waiting area of a gymnastics facility in Omaha, Nebraska. We had just moved back to Nebraska as a result of military assignment relocation. I began conversing with a woman seated next to me as we observed our daughters in the same gymnastics class. We probably talked about many things, but the only subject that I recollect (and will always be so grateful for) was piano instruction. She told me about Simply Music and then wrote down my name and telephone number so she could pass it on to a Simply Music teacher who lived very near us. This teacher, Janita Pavelka, called me a few days later and our lives have never been the same since!

My five-year-old daughter, Catherine, who had one and one-half years of piano using the Suzuki method, was the first one of my children to begin Simply Music. After a year, I then started my son, Trey, who is our oldest, in lessons.

By that time, I had become very familiar with the Simply Music method and had become friends with Janita.

I asked her if she would be willing to give Celeste lessons. She enthusiastically agreed and we began Celeste in a class with other students. Because the first class is an introductory session with a lot of verbal explanation, Celeste did not fare too well. It was too much language for her to focus on. After that first class, Janita suggested that she give Celeste private instruction, which has worked out beautifully.

In conducting Celeste's lesson, Janita treats her as she does any other student. Of course, some adaptations had to be made, but they are not always what one might expect. In Celeste's case, one of the biggest challenges is the Pavelka family dog, Dustin. Dustin is a very big, loud, and friendly chocolate Labrador who scares Celeste to death! Before she will enter the front door of the Pavelka house, she calls out, "No dog! No dog!" She is awaiting confirmation that Dustin is locked up in the basement before she enters the house.

Once she ascertains that Dustin is not going to surprise her, Celeste is ready for her lesson. In fact, she loves to go to her piano lesson and looks forward to it every week. Initially, she plays whatever song she is working on. Janita then guides and teaches Celeste the new material. Celeste is a very quick learner when it comes to piano and she has a very natural way of playing. This is quite amazing when you consider how difficult it is for Celeste to communicate. But when she sits down and plays piano, her fingers fly all over the keyboard and make the most beautiful music!

In piano lessons, Janita approaches Celeste just as she does any other student, though Celeste does not respond exactly the way other students do. In the beginning, Celeste's lessons had to be relatively short because she could not stay focused for very long. Now, her attention span and ability to follow instruction has greatly improved. We have no doubt that piano lessons have helped with this. Celeste is able to observe what Janita is teaching and follows her instructions. While at home, Celeste watches the DVD to review the new song she is learning. As she watches it, she learns from it just as my other children do. Having had no piano instruction, my husband and I are very grateful for those DVDs!

Effective Pattern Strategies

One of the wonderful things about the Simply Music method of learning piano is the way it teaches a song by having the student observe patterns on the keyboard. I think this is especially effective for visual learners, as most autistic individuals are. I was marveling during Celeste's lesson recently. It is amazing how a complicated song like Für Elise is separated into sections so that it can be learned at many levels. Each section is broken down into patterns so it is easily digestible. These patterns make the song easy to learn. I believe the Simply Music method is not only brilliant, but wonderfully tailored for people with developmental disabilities.

Celeste learns to play the Simply Music songs very quickly. She has a lot of natural ability and a very good ear for music. She also plays with a lot of feeling, which makes her playing so enjoyable to listen to. She transposes songs at will and she loves to make up her own songs. She has a spiral notebook filled with songs she has composed on our electronic piano, using different voices and styles. Every week, students are supposed to write four measures of music in 4/4 time, four measures of music in 3/4 time, and a stream of notes. This is for the reading rhythm part of the program. Celeste is able to write her measures and streams just like other students.

Blessing Others

At school, Celeste is noticed especially by the other students for her artistic ability and for her musical ability. At her school band concerts where she plays percussion, Celeste is openly smiling and happy, obviously enjoying the music she is playing. Parents have come up to us after the concerts to tell us how much they enjoy watching her play because she is usually smiling and genuinely enjoys playing in the band.

Her classmates and teachers have not had the opportunity to hear her play piano until recently. The thought came to me that it would be nice if Celeste could play piano for some of the teachers, perhaps after school. When I mentioned this to her teacher, there was a gleam in her eye and she suggested that she just might be able to arrange something for Teacher Appreciation Week. She arranged to have Celeste provide the background piano music for the teachers and staff of her school as they ate a specially prepared lunch in their honor. Celeste played many songs from her Simply Music playlist for a total of about an hour. There were three different thirty minute lunch periods for the teachers and she played for each one! Celeste's audience really seemed to enjoy her playing and it was a nice way to say, "Thank You," to the teachers for all their hard work.

Celeste really enjoys performing for others. Janita often arranges gigs at the local nursing homes for her students, to gain practice playing in public. The senior citizens have the pleasure of hearing and watching the children play music for them. They always seem to appreciate just having young people around! Celeste greatly enjoys all of these opportunities to play for others. We enjoy watching her smiling face and seeing her obvious heart-felt love of music.

These opportunities are wonderful for Celeste because they allow her the occasion to perform and they give others a chance to see how "fluent" she is in a different language.

A few months ago, we had to place my father-in-law in the Alzheimer's Unit at the Veteran's Home as my mother-in-law was no longer able to take care of him. Celeste and her siblings now get to play for their own grandfather when they visit. Celeste enjoyed playing for the folks there so much at the last visit, that if no one else was playing, she would jump up and start playing again.

Lately, Celeste has begun sitting down at the piano when her sister, Catherine, is practicing and she plays right along with her. It is wonderful to see Celeste, who normally prefers to do things alone, sitting alongside her sister playing the piano with her.

Janita schedules Simply Music recitals a couple of times a year and she encourages families to perform together as well as the students doing their own solo performances. Our family usually attempts playing a song together. I play guitar, my husband plays bass guitar, Catherine plays guitar, and we all sing. But we always have Celeste play accompaniment on piano for our family song. In spite of her autism, we *want* her to participate with us. And she is the best accompanist in the family!

Personal Growth

Because of her difficulties with language, one of the most frustrating things we have to contend with is trying to understand what Celeste thinks, feels, or wants. Her desires have become easier to figure out over time because she can say words, especially when it comes to asking for concrete things such as food items. Trying to figure out what she is thinking or feeling is still very difficult and sometimes very frustrating. My husband was so happy a few months ago when Celeste started saying, "Good morning, Dad!" when she came downstairs for breakfast. Prior to that, she would not acknowledge anyone's presence. Now she routinely greets us when she comes into the room or comes home from school. I know that there are probably several reasons why she is now doing this. I believe one of the reasons is because she plays the piano and performs for others.

Music is an important part of Celeste's life. We believe that good music is food for the soul; it brings us into union with our noblest selves as well as with Him who created us. Good music lifts our hearts and minds and makes us feel hopeful and happy. It would be a wonderful accomplishment if every person could learn to play a musical instrument. We chose piano for our children to learn first because on the piano, everything is laid out right in front of you. It's a good precursor to learning other instruments.

Simply Music is a wonderful way to learn to play piano. We love the philosophy of Simply Music; that music is a lifelong companion, meant to be a part of us until the day we die. To be able to sit down at a piano and play many songs from memory, to be able to improvise and compose, to be able to read lead sheets and accompany other musicians, and to be able to read music and play what is written, these are all the wonderful fruits of learning the Simply Music way.

We are so happy and eternally grateful to God for putting Simply Music into our path on our life journey. We are especially grateful because of what it has meant to Celeste. Life is not a race to be won; it is a journey to be traveled. We highly encourage anyone especially if you have a child with special needs to try Simply Music. It is ideal for those with extra difficulties in life, like Celeste. The Simply Music program certainly could have been designed just for them in mind. We know from personal experience that it works wonderfully.

We will always be grateful to Janita for being willing to work with Celeste and for teaching her to play the piano. She is so encouraging to the students and the parents. I remember when Janita predicted that Celeste will be a wonderful accompanist some day. That has given us great hope that Celeste might be able to find a way to use what she has learned for the good of others. Janita's departing admonition to the students each week at the end of lessons is, "Go forth into the world and be wonderful!" Good advice to us all.

§§§

I can't say enough about Simply Music. My grandson has been taking lessons for about four years. He has Aspergers Syndrome and has a hard time understanding what is said to him. Simply Music books enable him to see and understand what the numbers, signs, and arrows are telling him to do. His teacher is so very patient and highly trained to help him through any problem he might have. His fine motor and cognitive skills have improved. We are so thankful for Simply Music, making him proud of the things that he can do.

LuAnn Taylor, Parent
Salisbury, North Carolina

CHAPTER 13

A PERFECT
COMBINATION

The Benefits to the Homeschool Family

By Janita M. Pavelka
Kearney, Nebraska

Janita M. Pavelka, previously a traditional piano teacher, is now exclusively a Simply Music teacher. After teaching the Simply Music way for over six years, she can see the immense musical growth in her students, her children, and herself. She and her husband, Tim, homeschool their four children and play the piano along with various other instruments.

Something New In Our Lives

Homeschooling has been a way of life for my family for the past ten years and we love it! It has allowed our home to be the center of our family. It's given us the time to enjoy each other. We like being together at home and we enjoy the peace, privacy, and productivity that come with homeschooling. We enjoy the freedom of being ourselves without worrying about peer pressure. My children get one-on-one attention from me, the teacher, and I know exactly what they are learning and if they know it.

Something new has come into our lives in the last few years just as powerful to our family as homeschooling. Six years ago, a friend explained to me how Simply Music temporarily delays the music reading process. Students play great-sounding songs from their very first lessons. I dismissed it and didn't give it another thought until six months later when I saw a Simply Music ad in a reputable homeschool magazine. I gave the founder of Simply Music a call and my life has never been the same! From the beginning, Simply Music has become a primary force in our homeschooling.

When I was pregnant with our oldest child, I read a book entitled The Successful Home School Handbook: A Creative and Stress-free Approach to Homeschooling by Raymond and Dorothy Moore. What a difference it made for us! The Moore formula emphasized 1) Daily Study 2) Work and 3) Service, as part of the homeschool experience. We have applied this approach and it has changed our lives! We are happy that the Moores' well-rounded approach to study, work, and service fits so well with the well-rounded approach of Simply Music.

First, our academics include the four R's: reading, 'riting, 'rithmetic, and rhythm. Reading, writing, and math are all important skills in life. So is rhythm! The Simply Music method helps students to be musically self-expressed, just as a well-educated person is verbally and mathematically expressed.

Second, the amount of time spent working is equal to the amount of time spent book learning. For instance, if a kid spends four hours a day on his academics, he then spends four hours a day working on chores, his business, cleaning the house, running his paper route, working in the garden, working to learn a new skill, etc. This allows our children to live out what they learn. Understanding the value of work is important. Simply Music provides them the opportunity for such work, self discipline, and the pursuit of excellence.

Third, service is an important part of what we teach. All children tend to be naturally self-centered and egocentric. They can believe the world revolves around them. This perception can easily lead to a sense of entitlement. It is important to do service for others without expecting something in return. Children who do this grow up to be unselfish adults. Some of this service can include working in a local food pantry, volunteering at a pregnancy center, helping with the Salvation Army, and visiting the local retirement center. Simply Music provides the confidence to play and the immediate satisfaction of a job well-done for the sake of others.

Study

We can never study enough to master everything in this world. We can, however, teach our children the tools of learning and give them an on-going thirst for it. To be successful in our constantly changing world, we must be pliable, thirsty learners. Simply Music teaches us how to learn. There is a profound Simply Music premise which I believe is true: we are all musical beings.

When we study music, it opens up another world of knowledge. Rhythm brings a new dimension to learning which taps into a student's creativity and problem-solving abilities. Playing the piano the Simply Music way also stimulates the excitement of learning. This creates motivated learners who seek out their own education.

As parents, we want our children to love to learn. One of the benefits of homeschooling is that it opens up the world to life-long learning. Because Simply Music is such a fun way to learn the piano, students love to learn. Passions are pursued. Simply Music opens up the world of music and music as a life-long companion touches every area of our lives. It is never-ending.

Work

What's the point of doing school when you don't have the opportunity to make a difference with what you've learned? There is no point. Students who practice do perform better. Consistency in piano lessons also builds discipline and concentration, which produces commitment and perseverance, resulting in character and self-esteem. In Simply Music, students generally practice piano five times a week. Their efforts pay off when they are able to play their songs and see the fruit of their labors at the end of that week. Simply Music piano lessons are much more than just teaching the students how to play the piano. Many of the character qualities which are needed to excel in life are developed through this process of growth.

An additional outcome of Simply Music is that they can play their repertoire of songs, with both hands, anytime, anywhere, and for any reason. When they are able to play what they have practiced, they are using what they learn. My students perform publicly every month. They get to experience a sense of accomplishment and satisfaction that comes only from hard work. What a thrill it is for them!

On a different note, as a teacher of Simply Music, I show my children how I am using Simply Music as a meaningful, productive business. I model for them the value of business ownership. As a stay-at-home mom, I am able to homeschool my children in the daytime while teaching students in my home studio in the after-school hours. They see me taking risks, contributing to the family income, managing money, resolving conflicts, building relationships, and experiencing satisfied clients. What a great introduction to entrepreneurship!

Over the years, I continually talk with people about becoming Simply Music teachers. I'm convinced it is the best career they could have. For example, I asked a homeschool dad why he was paying me to teach his boys piano when he could be doing it himself. He didn't believe he could. I assured him he could easily learn how to be a Simply Music teacher and open his own studio. He signed up in June, opened his studio in August with twelve students, lost his job suddenly in October, and was very thankful he had the Simply Music income to rely on.

One of his major desires in life was to be a part-time pastor and help homeschool his children. His kids now have a pastor-dad who has joined his wife in homeschooling them. With his studio of twenty-five consistent students, he has been able to fulfill his dream. There are other homeschool dads who fully support their families by teaching Simply Music. They are not working forty to sixty hours a week away from their families. They are doing what they love, providing a good income for their family, homeschooling, and modeling for their children.

When we homeschool, we prepare our children to be productive citizens in the world. Simply Music has teachers as young as thirteen in the Teacher Training Program. These young teachers are learning how to make a living by developing their entrepreneurial skills. Having Simply Music as a viable career option can allow them to have a home business and make money while studying at home. It prepares them for life in a way that book work does not. Simply Music is a great alternative for them as they learn how to provide for their own future families.

Service

Service is a powerful part of every fulfilling lifestyle. It is important for each of us to learn how to give of ourselves. Simply Music provides students with the ability and opportunity to serve. Playing the piano at a nursing home, providing accompaniment for worship, using music to encourage, all allow students to focus on others. By learning to serve, our children's eyes are opened to a larger worldview, transforming their focus, making a difference in other people's lives. Learning this concept early in life allows our children to give back to the community and change the world.

This beautiful example of a homeschooled great granddaughter giving back, out of love and respect, is told by her mom:

My Grandmother loved to hear the kids play. The kids sharing the gift of music with Nana, which they learned through Simply Music, brought her so much joy at the end of her life amidst the suffering of terminal illness. It really is a testament to the fact that music is a gift that brings people together. On the day she died, when we received the call, we knew we had a chance to say good-bye to Nana. Not having the chance to say goodbye before someone dies can make us very sad. But, there we were with that chance! It was hard to know what to say and we were perplexed. So we prayed. And Mary Emma played.

Mary Emma always played the newest piece she had polished when we would call on Nana. It was just so ironic that her newest song was Home. *It really could not have been more perfect. Nana died just a few hours later. She went home.*

A Homeschool Happy Ending

I am glad we homeschool. I am glad that we have Simply Music, too. When I listen to my own four children play piano (my 'guinea pigs' from the beginning) I am reminded that I probably will never be able to transpose like them, play by ear as they can, or compose music and lyrics as they do. What a joy to know that choosing to homeschool our four children and having Simply Music piano as a main part of their schooling has enhanced their character and their impact on the world. They may not understand the contribution music is making to their lives, but they will when they are grown up. And they will thank us for it!

§§§

I have found Simply Music to be the ideal homeschool curriculum. It is flexible, creative, ground-breaking, and expansive. Ultimately, we are so proud that our son is blessing others because he is sharing his gift. Giving his talent away allows him to see the purpose in why he is learning piano in the first place. Whether it is for guests in our home, at our church, at the senior center, or anywhere there is a piano, he is always willing to play. It brings smiles to people's faces.

Mike Kirouac, Homeschool Parent
Sunnyvale, California

CHAPTER 14

REVERSAL OF ROLES

Wisdom of a Retiree

By *Adelaide De Medeiros*
San Jose, California

As a retired teacher, Adelaide De Medeiros fills her blissful days traveling, visiting with family and friends, gardening, reading, and, of course, playing the piano. She is a California state certified Portuguese interpreter and is an active member of Alpha Delta Kappa International Honorary Sorority for Women Educators. She is the very proud mother of two children.

The Budding Pianist

I grew up in the age of Rock-and-Roll. However, what I was listening to instead, what emboldened me to turn up the volume to the maximum allowed, was Beethoven's Fifth, Revel's Bolero, and Tchaikovsky's Nutcracker. While my sister grooved to American Bandstand, I pretended to conduct Henry Mancini's band. While this narrative unmasks me as a "seasoned" citizen, it serves to illustrate my early love of the classics and perhaps the genesis of my aspiration to someday play them myself. I waited a long time for that opportunity and that "someday" came closer and closer as I prepared to retire from a thirty-seven year teaching career. The day I retired, I took action.

The time and energy I had devoted to teaching French and history to middle school youngsters, in addition to raising a family, was about to be channeled in a new and exciting direction – the fulfilment of many dreams that had been held in check for a lifetime. Somewhere, I read that when women retire "they reinvent themselves". My reinvented self would emerge as a budding pianist!

I didn't approach retirement haphazardly. For some five years in advance, I had been collecting articles, resources, and ideas about what I wanted my new life to encompass. One resource that dropped into my lap, by way of some retired friends, was about an innovative and successful piano program that guaranteed anyone could learn to play the piano, from memory! Realistically, I knew full well that I didn't have a whole lifetime to develop my ability through a traditional program. This opportunity sounded like the ideal jump-start. Simply Music was the program they touted. They knew an instructor who was literally in my backyard. One year in advance of my retirement, I determined that the minute I was free, I would give Bernadette Ashby a call. When the day arrived in the summer of 2007, I did just that.

I suspect you might naturally wonder why this dream of mine, to be able to play the piano, had been so long in materializing. Suffices to say, my family had immigrated to the United States from Portugal when I was ten-years-old. Getting settled in a new land, half way across the world, was not an easy task. While higher education was definitely a priority in my parent's budget, piano lessons were not. Now in my methodic planning for retirement, I had navigated through the logic of including piano lessons in my own budgetary allocations. It fit perfectly into my file category of 'keep the grey matter growing/learn new things'.

Retiring to What?

Imagine this reversal of roles. I walked out of my classroom as a retired teacher and tiptoed right into a piano studio as a beginning student! Make no mistake; I was determine to be the kind of student I had always prayed for – one who was eager, enthusiastic, and diligent. I would have to make a concerted mental change from being a teacher to being a student!

In my previous life, I was so busy rushing around that I never noticed the numerical ratio of black keys to white keys on my instrument of choice! This was my starting point. Imagine my joy at coming home after my first lesson to practice a sequence of finger movements that actually sounded like music! Another two or three lessons and I was playing my very favorite of Beethoven's works, Ode to Joy! I find myself smiling from ear to ear, sometimes late at night, when I have successfully overcome a difficult part in a selection in progress.

The beauty of Simply Music is that when your lesson is over, you bring your instructor home with you on DVD, that is. There is never a risk of forgetting what I've learned, even if this aging mind wanted to. As an adult piano beginner, I naturally struggle. There is comfort in knowing that I can access the lesson visually as many times as I desire. It has helped me counteract any frustrations I've encountered.

To crown many of these private breakthroughs, I often pick up the phone and inflict my great accomplishments on my family members. Often I think back over the choice I made to learn piano versus learning to play golf, as some of my friends have. My advantage is I can play any time of day or night, as often as I want. This new pastime is a constant companion!

Shortly after I hunkered down to learn piano, one unexpected and delightful twist occurred in terms of my placement. The only group in the studio that was exactly at my beginning level just happened to be a collection of talented, effervescent, and adorable seven and eight-year-olds! I still remember my instructor's hesitation when she presented me with the proposal. How would I feel? Would I be comfortable? Would I 'fit in'? This was not standard practice.

Diplomatically, she hinted that students 'my age' didn't pick up the instruction as quickly as those other dynamic, young brains could. I'd have to be very diligent in order to keep up. My own take on this was that I had come this close to embarking on this lifelong dream and I wasn't about to balk at the challenge. I replied, "I've been a seventh grader all my life (remember, I was a thirty-seven year veteran of the middle school). It'll feel like home."

Instantly, I was reaping the benefits of this 'cross-age' experiment. For starters, by design, I would be last in the group rotation. I was comfortable with this. It gave me the opportunity to see the work at hand, modeled and corrected several times, before I had to demonstrate mastery. In this respect, I have the advantage of staying focused 100% of the time. My young classmates, programmed to manifest their age-appropriate kinesthetic propensity, are more likely to lose the necessary focus. It works out to everyone's advantage. I admire their fearless ability to jump in and perform new tasks, or to improvise, or compose without any doubt or hesitation. They have always shown the utmost respect for this 'older version' of themselves. And our instructor has told me how much the parents love having a 'more mature and wise student' in the class. Some very special bonds have been forged.

Overcoming Fears

I am in deep gratitude to one of these "cherubs" for my greatest musical epiphany since starting Simply Music. As an adult, I know that many fears can hinder the learning process. We bring in our own set of expectations, insecurities, and failures into whatever situation we are facing. If we allow them to, they can overtake opportunities for growth. As silly as it may sound, my struggle in learning to play the piano came in the form of 'using the pedal'. Until being instructed to do so, I had never used the sustain (right) pedal. When it came time to practice at home, I found that the loud, runaway sound was more than I could tolerate. I rationalized that my forty-year-old Wurlitzer must need some adjustment and so I opted to use the left pedal instead. One thing I could appreciate early on was the beautiful sound of my teacher's grand piano. My piano didn't even come close to the full, rich sounds that I could produce at her studio.

Then came the day, when young Jonathan, our group's most daring composer of lively music, came to visit. I promptly invited him to play and I couldn't believe my ears. Jonathan brought my Wurlitzer to life! He made it sound like a grand. I was baffled. I noticed that this young pianist worked the right pedal expertly. When he left, I tested out the fearsome appendage, determined to overcome this challenge whatever the price. My jaw dropped. Then I grinned from ear to ear. For the first time since I bought the piano, my music sounded rich and full as if it were from a more sophisticated specimen. I wanted to play all night as I heard each song from my repertoire come alive! By watching Jonathan model for me the accessibility and the beauty of the sound from the pedal, I was inspired and overcame my fear of using it. This victory gave me the confidence needed to overcome other challenges.

My Contribution

Once a teacher, always a teacher. My unofficial role in the studio is to bridge our studio learning experience with music in the real world. I have been dubbed the 'studio educator'. For example, when an exhibit entitled Schulz Beethoven: Schroeder's Muse came to the local university's Beethoven Center, I brought it to the studio's attention and arranged for a group tour. My young classmates got the thrill of their lives when the curator actually allowed them to play one of the precursors to our modern piano! The same can be said for scouting news of local performances. I'm also inclined to share news about great musicians and composers. I am contributing once again in another area which I love. How fulfilling it is for me to give back.

Noticing Music

When I originally set out to include learning to play the piano as one of my goals for retirement, I had certain expectations. As I look back, the rewards far exceed those original expectations. Some of these have been delightfully surprising. For instance, I was absolutely tickled when I came to a passage I read in a novel, Amazing Disgrace.[1] The main character, a food critic, says this,

---

1   Hamilton-Paterson, James, Amazing Disgrace, Europa Editions, New York, 2006, page 49.

"For me, dishes involving these particular three foods come to the table in the keys of D flat, B minor, and F sharp respectively." Before piano lessons, this would have gone right over my head. But as I read and reread the passage with sheer enjoyment, I was able to visualize exactly where these keys are located. In my mind, I even heard their sound. I chalked up another benefit of delving into piano. Music is all around us and I am noticing it.

In another work called Leeway Cottage,[2] a passage explained how the main character as a young child had learned to play by ear. "Mr. Moss' music he learned by reading note by note, often astonished when he heard what those notes, all like random black bugs that had died all over the page, connoted as sound. The music he played by ear was spacious and three dimensional, with structures and rooms like castles of sound, while the Chopin was as flat as a map." It was as if the author were describing Simply Music and the beauty of self-expression! This book I promptly tucked into my piano bench as a keeper. As I reflect on the fact that I delayed piano playing until my golden years, I indeed found a treasure, to be able to make beautiful music immediately instead of "typing" my way through pieces, thanks to Simply Music.

Like most individuals, I'm 'wired' for certain music preferences while resisting others. With Simply Music, I'm learning to appreciate genres I would never have considered. Because I am a beginning music student, I can now engage in conversations about such things as chords with my young teen-age nephew and a young neighbor. Both are beginning guitarists. I might add that I have their total admiration. They are a captive audience when I play!

2   Gutcheon, Beth, Leeway Cottage, Harper Perennial, New York, 2006, page 302.

Finally, as I embark on the journey of reading notes, I will hit another one of my expectation 'bench marks'. That is, being able to decode this new mysterious secret language of music. I am thrilled at the prospect. So far, the transition to reading music has been as natural as breathing. The sum total of the above rewards is that I am even more committed to expanding my knowledge of piano.

When I first started, I questioned whether I could become a pianist. But without a shadow of a doubt, I know with each successful lesson, it is becoming a reality. Simply Music has made it possible for anyone at any age to succeed at playing the piano. It has enriched my new life every day, even if it meant a humbling reversal of roles.

§§§

Now that I am retired, I can devote my full attention to music. I have much more than twenty minutes a day to devote to this. Having been the principal trombone player for the Ventura County Symphony from 1962 to 1977, I know the importance of mastering material before moving on. I can see why this approach could be so successful for beginners. I can see where persons with my kind of background could use this approach to great advantage.

Rene Rodriguez, Student, Age: 70
Newbury, California

CHAPTER 15

PIANO FUN

Adding that Playful Touch

By *Mary Robertson*
Huntington Woods, Michigan

Mary E. Robertson sang for twenty years with the Michigan Opera Theatre. She holds an M.A. in teaching and is a certified K-5 teacher in Michigan. For fun, she's chosen to teach Kindermusik, theatre arts classes, and, of course, Simply Music. As a mother of two girls, she likes to read, stare at Lake Michigan, and make people laugh.

Boring?

A full page newspaper ad displays some young hotshots doing impressive snowboard moves on a hill covered in deep, fresh powder. The caption reads: "Would you rather be doing this or taking boring piano lessons?" Hmmm...boring piano lessons? Who says they have to be *boring*?

We know that Simply Music makes piano accessible to folks of all ages who thought they'd never play piano. We know that Simply Music removes a huge barrier by postponing the reading process. We know that Simply Music gives people self-affirmation through immediate success; playing real songs with both hands. But wait! Is piano even supposed to be fun? Parents want their children to learn discipline, to build skills, to have a musical background. Can we do all this and still have our children enjoy it?

Simply Music teachers have the goal of making music a life-long companion for each and every one of their students. This objective works best within an atmosphere that promotes fun! Making piano lessons playful is critical to achieving our goals. By making piano accessible, engaging, self-affirming, and just plain fun, Simply Music increases by ten-fold the chance that students will stick with it long enough for it to become part of the fabric of their lives, something so ingrained that it is permanent. What a gift to give our children! What a joy to be able to do that for them.

You don't necessarily have to be crazy to bring a playful touch to piano lessons. But it certainly helps to have a screw or two loose! The structure and philosophy of the Simply Music method make it easy to experience piano lessons as a joyful and maybe even an occasionally silly event. Here are some of the reasons why.

Playing Songs Right Away

I once picked up my daughter at a friend's house where the piano was right in the entryway. I asked how the lessons were going and the Mom replied, "Not great." I looked at the open book on the piano. The child was being asked to play one hand only to a catchy little tune that went like this, "This is Mr. C," while pounding middle C. "This is Mr. G, Mr. C, Mr. G." Similar pounding. In contrast, the Simply Music method focuses on music making right away.

A Simply Music student from their very first lessons will be taught a song called <u>Dreams Come True</u>, a lovely little ballad with engaging lyrics. Students are so excited because they can play a song with both hands after a lesson or two. Kids come to piano lessons because they want to play songs on the piano, songs that are pleasurable. With Simply Music, playing is instantaneously rewarding.

Evolving Team Spirit

The pressure to perform in a one-on-one lesson can be intense. Students may feel a need to please the teacher, may be afraid to make mistakes, and may even be concerned that they don't know how to do it "right". Simply Music encourages group lessons where students can watch and learn several times before being expected to play themselves. The atmosphere has a cheerleader-like excitement with a team spirit evolving in the group. The weekly gathering becomes a social event. Students may work together on patterns, model how to play songs, figure out ways to describe chords, and, often times, encouraging words abound. Parents may even exchange practice ideas.

Because of the group dynamics, it's also easier to incorporate musical games into the lesson. For example, we often play a 'stump your classmate game' where one student asks another to play a certain song or create a certain chord. The challenges can get pretty difficult. E# 13 is my personal favorite chord! Another fun game of chance is called 'playlist review'. Students can pull color-coded popsicle sticks or roll dice to determine which songs are to be played from their repertoire. The tic-tac-toe game (class versus teacher) gets even more entertaining as the teacher gets a square every time a student cannot start a song correctly. I almost always lose, happily! The group setting allows for effective game playing. The focus on building repertoire makes the game playing possible. Piano class can be a thrilling experience and good memories are made with friends!

A Lifelong Companion

Have you ever willingly chosen a companion that didn't bring you joy? Music should be no different. An achievement-driven, pressure-cooker atmosphere in piano lessons where the ultimate goal is concert level performance can produce more anxiety than smiles. Consider another option.

Because Simply Music has an entirely different philosophy, it can emphasize the joy along the way; being able to play an impressive number of songs in a few short weeks, exploring creativity through composition and improvisation, and participating in ensemble play through the accompaniment program. Simply Music students *want* to go to the piano because they experience music making as an uplifting, self-affirming, joyful experience.

The piano can also become an instrument where life experiences express a full range of emotions. For example, when I'm happy, I'll play Amazing Grace in every key and sing at the top of my lungs. Or after experiencing the loss of a friend, I went to the piano and played Tear for a Friend. When my kids hear Ballade. a fast paced classical piece. they know that I'm mad. What a fantastic way to release all that tension. They are certainly relieved!

Imagine coming home from work. It's been a stressful day and you would rather not watch the evening news. So after dinner, you spend the next few hours unwinding by playing the piano. Your repertoire of hundreds of songs is at your disposal. All of life's cares are taken away. Tension is released and relaxation takes over. Time flies. Knowing these benefits, wouldn't it be worthwhile to focus on making music a life-long companion? That's the goal in Simply Music – to make music a friend till the day we die.

Performance Opportunities

Recital horror stories abound. The pressure to perform is intense. Many a promising student has thrown in the musical towel to avoid the anxiety of formal recitals. My sister has become immortalized as I tell every class in my studio (with her permission) about the time she forgot her recital piece in the middle of a song. She stopped dead in her tracks and walked to the middle of the stage. In a dramatic voice, she sniffled, "I'm sorry, I cannot go on." Then she sashayed off the stage.

Most Simply Music teachers offer a free-flowing alternative to the standard recital, called a Piano Party. Students come, with or without family members, and play for each other. They are inspired by the playing of others, happy at having shared their own gifts, enjoy refreshments, and go home feeling fulfilled and satisfied. Adult students have their own Piano Party. Sometimes, it is in the form of an intimate 'wine and cheese' party with a no-pressure atmosphere to perform.

New Venues

The average piano student works on one piece at a time, playing it at a recital, and possibly never again. Simply Music students have a large enough repertoire in the first three months to give a mini-concert in any available venue. I tell vacationing students to find a piano at a ski lodge or on a cruise ship. They might ask the person in charge for permission to play and put a small jar labelled 'college fund' on the piano. There is nothing more irresistible than an adorable kid playing piano. It's true!

Students can learn Tear for a Friend because we never know when someone might need a pianist for a funeral. When we learn Star Spangled Banner, I remind them that I am an opera singer and that any day now the call will come in for me to sing at a major league sporting event. They need to be prepared to accompany me at Comerica Park or Joe Louis arena here in Detroit! When we learn about transposition in the accompaniment program, I tell them that Aunt Bertha can't sing Amazing Grace in this key. Then I do an imitation of her saying in a high old lady voice, "Sonny, Aunt Bertha's voice just won't go that high!" To which the student is trained to reply, "No problem. Let me just change the key for you!" When they ask who Aunt Bertha is, I tell them everybody has an Aunt Bertha, or Uncle Fred, or Grandma Susie who might want to sing along at family gatherings.

Music Exploration

Sometimes, we are more restricted than we know. Classical music is wonderful, but it may not speak to everyone. Even though I've been a life-long singer, I could never accompany myself. Before I discovered Simply Music I knew nothing about the blues. Simply Music opens up the entire musical world, exploring varied genres of music.

Exploration of the blues, in particular, provides several opportunities for a playful approach. For example, we have new words for Jackson Blues, retitled The Homework Blues:

Oh my teacher gave me WAY too much to do,
That's why I'm singin', singin' the Homework Blues, oh yeah!

As a Simply Music teacher, I have the freedom to express my own light-heartedness through the blues. My favorite light-hearted moment when teaching the blues to students is discussing the need for the left hand pinky (number five finger) to keep jumping and striking the low C in Jackson Blues. This is a challenge for most kids since this particular song requires an active pinky. When the pinky inevitably stays put, I stop the song and ask if I could have a private moment with that finger. I hold the pinky in my hand, address it directly, and yell, "Jump!" while the class laughs. I then tell the student that this will take some work and may involve feeding the pinky a new diet of spinach and brussels sprouts, taking it for special sessions on a trampoline, or possibly purchasing a set of teeny, tiny barbells. They think this is hysterical, but they almost always come back the next week with a lively pinky!

Begging to Read

After a year or so of lessons when students have a huge repertoire and feel great about their playing, they are introduced to reading. They usually beg and plead to have this new skill added to their bag of musical tricks. They are so excited at the prospect. Already, they have been reading chords for many months. There is nothing scary for them about taking instruction from the page.

The Simply Music approach of separating rhythm and notes, makes reading even more fun and accessible. Through 'Masters of the Rhythm' exercises, the group claps and plays at increasing speeds, trying to show their mastery of the rhythm patterns that are key to understanding music. As the speed increases, mistakes are made. There is lots of laughter along the way.

Teacher Happy Dance

A bit of silliness occurs on the occasion when a student (or class) does something truly extraordinary; everybody can play all their songs perfectly, or has mastered a difficult song, or everyone has written remarkable compositions, etc. At these times, I do the 'teacher happy dance' which consists of me standing up and making very fast foot and arm movements, looking like a crazy person. They usually laugh pretty hard, but also recognize they have done something special.

There are plenty of opportunities for the Simply Music teacher to inject light-heartedness into lessons. I say snowboarding is nothing compared to a great piano lesson that includes the wonders of musical self-expression and the joy of a good laugh!

§§§

After teaching piano using traditional methods for over thirty years, I was blown away to discover Simply Music. I am very relieved that I will no longer 'lose' students because they are bored with the slowness of learning or totally frustrated with struggling to read and me constantly saying, "Keep your eyes on the page." I have been introduced to a gift that is so precious and is so much fun!

Marg Green, Simply Music Teacher
Gowrie, ACT, Australia

CHAPTER 16

A HUSBAND'S
CONSENSUS

Agreeing to the Business

By Jacob Lozier
Rochester Hills, Michigan

Jacob Lozier loves his family. He and Carrie are the proud parents of three-year-old Aeden. Jacob has several degrees in engineering and masters in Business Administration. He has been working for General Motors for nearly ten years in various developmental and leadership roles.

Anxiety

I heard the tick, tick, ticking away of the timer. Mom stood in the kitchen making dinner, while I was anxiously sitting in front of the old upright piano. Its front panels were missing, the stain removed, and several keys were broken. I probably shouldn't mention that it had never been tuned. In less than fifteen minutes, my piano teacher would arrive for lessons. This was the first time I sat at the piano since last week's lesson. I knew I hadn't practiced. So now I crammed my playing in. I was frustrated and disheartened. Hating my piano books at the moment, I was dreading the arrival of the nice gray-haired teacher that would soon knock on the door.

For more than a year, such was my experience with the piano. I was twelve and playing goofy songs with one hand, writing in the letters of every note with the other. I did learn enough in those lessons to help me advance as a trumpet player. But it was not the positive experience I am sure my parents hoped it would be. Twenty years later, I still look back at those lessons and cringe, praying my son will never have such an experience. Over the years, I have developed a love for music, but to this day I still cannot play a song on the piano.

Lover of Music

My wife, Carrie, however, has played music since she was very young. Her love for music is in her blood. She has spent thousands of hours 'tickling the ivory' with her fingertips and holding a cello bow in her hand. Her career began as a piano teacher in high school when a family friend asked if she would teach their twins. Since then, she graduated with a degree in piano performance. For the past twenty years, she has taught hundreds of children and adults.

We met in June 2003 and I soon discovered her love of music. One thing that stood out about her is her deep desire to share music with anyone she could. We were soon married and our life together began. Carrie was teaching at a music school, but quit in order to start her own studio. It was during a lesson that a parent introduced her to a revolutionary Australian playing-based method called Simply Music.

As we investigated Simply Music and poured over their claims, we were both interested and challenged. Carrie spent hours looking into this method; reading the website, researching information, combing the testimonials, and comparing the results to her own teaching. Most intriguing was how the method began. It was developed by Neil Moore for an eight-year-old blind boy. It seemed that Simply Music had the potential for anyone to learn how to play the piano, including those with learning challenges. It was obvious that Carrie was getting excited about revising her teaching approach. Simply Music ideally paves the way for her to successfully share her true love for music with her students.

Cost Concerns

Our biggest concern, however, was the license and training cost. It caused us to think twice. It was a lot of money for anyone to spend, but as newlyweds it seemed a bit much. Additionally, when Carrie discussed the potential methodology change with some of her students, their response was mixed.

Carrie contacted Simply Music for more information. She had several calls discussing the method with Neil Moore, the creator of Simply Music. We weighed out all the pros and cons of starting a new business venture. Because of Simply Music's focus on group lessons, a Simply Music teacher could potentially double, triple, quadruple the amount of income generated over the average piano teacher. This was appealing to us. In the end, despite the cost and the potential loss of nearly 25% of her students, the decision was easy. I wholeheartedly agreed to this new business venture. Carrie realized that teaching traditional piano lessons has its frustrations. She was more than willing to give this up. It was time for a change and Simply Music was the breath of fresh air she needed.

Studio Success

That decision was made over six years ago. Carrie now has a studio of seventy students ranging from six years of age to seventy-five. As I look back, the initial cost of starting a Simply Music business was minimal when compared to the results we've achieved. The most amazing thing is that most of Carrie's students willingly transitioned to Simply Music. Now, I had a new concern, "How do we handle the parking?" However, this is not what kept me up at night. I've really only told half of the story. I was working as an engineer for General Motors. I thought it was the dream job – great pay and benefits and it gave us more than we needed financially to live comfortably. Carrie's studio was doing well as she taught Simply Music. We had a fantastic life!

Family Business

My life (and perceptions) changed three-and-a-half years ago when our son, Aeden, was born. Instead of wanting to spend more time at work solving a challenging problem, I wanted to be home with him and to teach him how important each moment can be. This desire has only grown over the years. My employer was experiencing some of the darkest hours of their corporate history. The recession had hit and my job stability was unsure. Fortunately, I was able to maintain my position at General Motors. That experience helped me to focus on what was important in life. Today, I stay pretty busy as a husband, father, handyman, landscaper, and Design Engineer, still at General Motors. But change is on the horizon.

During a recent frustrating situation at work, I found myself praying for change. I soon realized that everything we had been through and learned together was preparing us, as a family and as individuals, for something new. In the past two years of the recession, Carrie's Simply Music studio had experienced more than 60% growth in student enrollment. This growth was contrary to the economy at large. It is not characteristic of traditional piano studios. Simply Music has allowed Carrie to accomplish much more with the Simply Music method than she may have without it.

So, I reminded her of a dream she shared several years ago – to open a studio for music education that was different, that stood out. As a recent MBA graduate, I had been learning about marketing, finances, and making the right decisions in difficult markets. We decided that together we could manage a studio. I would run the business and Carrie could train teachers and maintain a teaching schedule. This allowed her to expand her reach to share music throughout our community.

It has been several months since this decision has been made. We have been discussing this and researching endlessly. I expect that our lives will be crazy for a while as Carrie maintains her home studio and I continue to work at a job I can't really stand. Our hope is that we will develop a new business model that will not only support our family, but will become the leading music studio in our area. The goal is to help our students develop a lifelong relationship with music. We believe that this altruistic focus will lend to a satisfying career for both of us. Carrie's studio growth has shown us that Simply Music works, is lucrative, and that it will continue to give us the freedom we want with our time.

Simply Music has changed our lives, allowing possibilities which I believe would not have been possible otherwise. Carrie loves to teach! She loves to share her love for music. Simply Music gives her the avenue in which to do so. As her business manager, I am her biggest supporter and fan. The benefits are worth it as I look forward to being home more with her and Aeden, building a business, and raising our family together. Who knows? I might just go back and take up piano lessons again.

§§§

Simply Music is great! It has allowed my wife to do something that she loves. It is financially beneficial, too. In the beginning, I was hesitant because it was a new method, a new concept, and new to our area. I don't know much about music, but she believed in it so passionately that I agreed to the business. We have seen great success and it has allowed her the freedom to not only own her business, but to make her own schedule. I look forward to the future and the opportunities that Simply Music brings.

Hunter Thorpe, Spouse to Robin Thorpe (Simply Music Teacher) Franklin, Tennessee

CHAPTER 17

THE SHARED LESSON ADVANTAGE

Why Group Lessons Work

By Kerry Hanley
Balwyn North, Victoria, Australia

Kerry Hanley is a classically trained pianist and has studied both voice and double bass. She is a graduate of the Certificate of Music (in Jazz) program at the Western Australia Academy of Performing Arts. She has been teaching piano since 1989 for the first nine years using a more traditional method. After seeing the benefits, she immediately changed all of her students over to the Simply Music approach and saw results, unlike anything she'd ever witnessed. Kerry is a Senior Associate Teacher and a Senior Trainer and conducts Teacher Workshops around Australia.

"Most things we do in life, we do in groups." Neil Moore
'Shared Lessons' are a dynamic and effective way to teach and to learn. We all learn better in groups. We are born into a group – our families. We receive most of our education in groups – either in schools or in home schooling and in

college or university. We work in groups, we play in groups, and we worship in groups.

Yet for centuries, piano has largely been taught on an individual basis. Therefore, students, parents, and teachers frequently show some initial reluctance or nervousness about the idea of Shared Lessons. They mistakenly assume that individual attention by the teacher produces a better quality result. In fact, the opposite is often true. This essay demonstrates why.

The following characters are fictional, but their stories are not. These stories are typical of real teachers, parents, and students in the Simply Music program who have experienced the Shared Lesson advantage.

THE CHILDREN

The Lessons

Reuben and his mum walk down the path to a big room at the back of the house. She knocks on the door of the piano studio for Reuben's first lesson. The Simply Music Teacher, Melissa, answers the door with a big smile and warm welcome that they remembered from the first time they met her. Reuben is excited and also a little nervous. He can't wait to learn to play the songs that Melissa demonstrated at the Introductory Session. His heart is beating fast and he feels a little shy, "What will it be like to learn with the other kids? Will it be fun? Will I like them? Will it be as easy as it seemed?"

The other students and their parents are there already and so Melissa asks them to introduce themselves to each other. There are four kids – Reuben, Becca, Sasha, and Tristan. They each have a parent with them, who must also attend all the lessons. Melissa had explained to the parents before the lesson that they wouldn't be doing anything on the keyboard in their first session, so they are not surprised. She shows them how to use the Student Home Materials and describes how the lessons will flow. She lets them know what is expected of them both in the lesson and at home.

There is only one piano for the four kids. Melissa has them stand in a semi-circle around the piano with the parents standing behind them. "When we are learning something new, you will take turns at being the 'volunteer' at the piano." Melissa explains, "Sometimes, we may do a 'round-robin' where each of you take turns to quickly try a little of something we have learned, such as a chord progression. It could be playing a chord like this." As each student sits down at the piano, Melissa pushes their hands onto the keyboard to play any ten keys at the same time, in a mock version of playing a chord. It sounds terrible. Everyone laughs. They begin to relax.

Melissa hands out their Student Home Materials. As they open their packages, it looks like Christmas morning. Children and parents alike are excited and their faces are beaming. They can't wait to start learning a song next week.

Second Lesson

The next Tuesday comes quickly. The students have been listening at home to the CD of the songs they will be learning in Level One. They are keen to get started.

Melissa asks everyone to come around the piano. After telling them the finger numbers, they play a game to learn them. Melissa calls out the finger number for them to show and with each round she purposely gets faster and faster, till no one can keep up. They all laugh.

After learning some more basics, they all go back to their seats and begin to learn some patterns in their fingers for the first song. Once everyone can demonstrate the sentences in the air with their fingers, Melissa asks them to come back up to the piano. She asks Reuben to be the 'volunteer' on the keyboard. He is very enthusiastic. As Melissa gently guides him to play the sentences they just learned, everyone else is crowding around the piano and watching. They can clearly see what Reuben is doing. As Reuben begins to play, they hear the sentences they have just learned being translated onto the piano. Their faces light up as they recognize them as the first song. Melissa acknowledges him and he feels proud of himself. The parents are beaming also – they can't believe it! They are amazed that it could be so easy to learn to play a song. The parents start to realize that even they could go home and play the song too! None of them have tried it on the piano yet – but they don't need to – they have learnt *'how to learn'* the song. All they need to do is practice it. Some of the kids and parents wonder if they will remember what to practice, until Melissa reminds them to review the DVD in the Student Home Materials when they get home, to ensure they are doing it correctly during the week.

Third Lesson

With everyone crowding around the piano, they take turns at showing a little of what they have been practicing at home. They feel very pleased with themselves. Melissa praises the students for their success. Sasha has a little pause before some of the notes, so Melissa gently clarifies how to play without gaps. Everyone can see the coaching Melissa is giving. When Tristan plays, he also plays with some pauses, but now he knows how to fix it at home. Becca plays a little too fast, so Melissa encourages her to slow down. Hearing each other play helps them to notice the differences between what they are doing and what their teacher has demonstrated.

Melissa introduces a new song. She shows them the right hand for the first half of the song. Everyone – students and parents alike – put the patterns into their fingers in the air before coming to the piano. Tristan volunteers to be the first to try it. He makes a small mistake, so Melissa explains the correction and the second time he does it correctly. The others see not only what to do, but also what mistakes to avoid.

Next, Melissa instructs Tristan what to do in the left hand and how to put the first section hands together. This time, instead of doing a round-robin, Melissa asks everyone to return to their seats to use the paper keyboards – the 'Practice Pads'. Each student uses a Practice Pad and works with their parent. First, the students try it with their parent watching and mentoring, and then they swap. The kids giggle at the role-reversal. Now their parents are the students and the kids are the mentors. Everyone is engaged and having fun. While mentoring, the kids are reinforcing the patterns they have learned. With no sound to rely on, it deepens their understanding of the patterns.

Fourth Lesson

All week, the kids are looking forward to seeing each other. Some of them arrive early and go into the practice room next door to show each other what they can play. Becca has a question about the song, so the others mentor her.

When the previous group leaves, they go into the main room and the lesson begins. Sasha is the shy one in the group and had not previously volunteered. But she was able to watch, relax, and absorb everything the others were doing. Her success has boosted her confidence and now she is inspired! This time when Melissa asks for volunteers, Sasha wants to show off what she has achieved.

Reuben is also excited to play a piece of music he has made up himself. Melissa praises him profusely and the others get inspired to try composing something themselves during the week. Reuben's piece gives them some ideas and the confidence to give it a try.

After some review and coaching, they are ready to learn a new song. Becca volunteers and Melissa shows her a three-chord progression using the chords they learned in their second lesson. Becca copies, then the group does a round-robin game. They each try, quickly one after the other, to play those three chords. They move so fast, the energy is high, and by the end everyone is laughing. Melissa shows quickly and easily how to turn this into their first blues song. Everyone is blown away! It really sounds like the blues – and they've only had four lessons! They can't wait to get home and try it! There's a bubble of excitement as they leave. The kids bounce out the door laughing together while the parents follow up behind chatting about the great results so far. Their shared experience of success deepens the friendships that are forming between the kids and between the parents. There's a camaraderie they didn't quite expect.

Twelfth Lesson

This week, the students learn a complex rhythm for a blues song they are about to learn. They drum the rhythm on their laps. First they do it all together, then one by one.

This way, they can more easily hear if they haven't quite got the rhythm right yet. Melissa leads them to drum the rhythm faster and faster, till no one can keep up. There's a cacophony of sound and everyone dissolves into laughter.

Reuben and Becca tend to get the songs down a little more quickly than the other two and sometimes need more of a challenge. Melissa senses this, so she spends a few minutes toward the end of the lesson, showing a more advanced version – called an 'Arrangement' – of one of the songs they've already learned. Naturally, Sasha and Tristan are watching too, but they don't have to learn the Arrangement until they are ready. They are unconsciously picking up some of it ahead of time and later Reuben and Becca can mentor them on how to play it.

The kids have become quite comfortable playing in front of each other. They are used to playing even when the song is not perfect or complete, while it was still evolving. They don't even realize that they are learning valuable lessons in sharing their music with others. Becca's mum casually mentions that Becca volunteered and played one of her pieces at a school assembly last Thursday in front of two hundred people! Becca's mum smiles with pride – their house is already filled with music and she is thrilled because her daughter is playing and they are singing together. All the students are composing their own music at home and have also explored some improvising. They have twelve songs in their repertoire including blues, classical, contemporary, accompaniments, and arrangements – which they can play from memory, without the aid of music.

The relationships that are developing among the students spill over outside of class. Sometimes they even meet together to practice and the sounds of duets abound. They are learning how to play music with others and are at the same time becoming good friends. They have begun to socialize on weekends and after school.

The parents are pleased with the positive group interaction. They are grateful for the support of the other parents and students. By being involved in Shared Lessons, they get to witness the progress of not just their own child, but also the other kids and they share in the joy of each child's achievements. They are all grateful for this special time and connection with their children that they don't ordinarily get in their day-to-day activities. They wouldn't change it for the world.

THE ADULTS

Introductory Session

Esme knocks on the music studio door for the Introductory Session. A kind-looking man in his mid-forties greets her and introduces himself as John, the Simply Music teacher. He invites her into the studio and she sits down next to a gentleman who looks about her age. Esme is relieved and buoyed to see other adults there. It gives her hope. She has wanted to be able to play the piano since she was a young girl, but her parents couldn't afford lessons. Now some of her friends think she might be too old. Perhaps they are wrong and finally her dreams can be fulfilled. There's a sense of expectancy in the room and everyone is keen to hear what John has to say.

"Most of the things we do in life, we do in groups. Sports, dance classes, research projects, all work better in groups. I was a beginning student myself only a few years ago and I learned in a group," began John. "I teach a variety of ages, but half my students are adults. The oldest student I've taught was in his nineties."

151

Esme is aghast. Compared to that, in her sixties, she's a spring chicken! She can feel herself relaxing. Another gentleman pipes up, "It's been fifty years since I've touched a piano and I wasn't that good at it then. I want you to show me that it's not too late for me to learn."

"Alright then, let's get on with it." John does some strange things with his hands, "middle to top, top to bottom, bottom to middle…" It doesn't make a lot of sense to Esme, but she copies him with her fingers anyway. When he sits down at the piano, she instantly recognizes Beethoven's <u>Ode to Joy</u>. She is astonished! At the first opportunity, she signs up to begin the lessons – she is determined to prove her friends wrong – she is *not* too old!

First Lesson

John asks for a volunteer from one of the eight adult students and Esme steps up to the piano. What does she have to lose? Her fingers don't work as well as they used to, but she's hoping that piano practice might ease the arthritic pain. As she pushes down and lifts her fingers from the keyboard, the other students encourage her. They understand the challenge she is overcoming. She feels like she has someone cheering her on for the first time in a long time. By the end, they're all laughing together. There's an energy in the room and a level of ease that Esme usually only feels with old friends. She could get used to this.

Three Months Later

Esme looks forward to coming early every week to chat with the other people in the group. Sometimes they meet together socially for a cup of coffee or a meal. She loves her class! Everything she had hoped for in learning to play the piano is coming true. But just as importantly, she feels connected to others again. This session they are going to practice together for the student concert they're doing this weekend at the senior residence down the street. It's a running joke in the group – their average age is probably older than the people they will be playing for.

Esme married in her mid-twenties and had three children. She loved the life she devoted to her husband and children, but there was very little 'Esme' time. Now Esme has a large repertoire of songs and loves to play the piano. Her grandchildren love to hear her play and they sit with her and try to play, too. What a joy to share her love of music with them! She's giving them an interest in the piano – a bonus that she hadn't anticipated. At sixty-three, life is fun!

THE TEACHER

In her quiet way, Melissa smiles once again. There are so many things to be grateful for. Her part-time income as a teacher supplements their household finances. She spends more time with her family because she is only teaching a few hours a week. Lessons are different every time. No boredom here! And how much she has learned through the Shared Lessons experience about relationships and the benefits of learning in a group.

She's contributing something to the world, making it a better place. She knows that she is making a difference and that gives her a quiet confidence and patience with her own family. Shared Lessons contribute to her personal fulfillment and satisfaction.

The Shared Lesson experience has changed lives. Children and adults have learned to love to make music along the way. Shared Lessons work! They are a benefit to students, parents, and teachers alike. Melissa has a choice to teach shared or private lessons and there is no question what she would do! Group learning, after all, is the best way to learn.

THE SHARED LESSON ADVANTAGE FOR STUDENTS
Observatory Learning:

- ♦ More effective use of lesson time
  - ♦ When one person gets coaching, everyone gets the coaching
  - ♦ Teacher doesn't need to 'watch' the students practice to ensure a good result
- ♦ Less intimidating
  - ♦ Ability to 'hide' and observe first
  - ♦ Students can be relaxed and absorb more
- ♦ Learning from each other
  - ♦ Questions that you wouldn't have thought to ask yourself
  - ♦ Learning from mistakes of others – what to avoid for the future
- ♦ Inspired by what others are achieving
  - ♦ One student's progress can show others what is possible
  - ♦ Inspires each other's creativity
- ♦ Room for progressing at different rates
  - ♦ Ideas for faster students, that others can observe for when they are ready

Participatory Learning:
- Experiential, dynamic, interactive
- Gaining experience in playing in front of others
  - Not about producing concert pianists
  - Fosters philosophy 'music is to be shared'
  - Develops ease in playing for others,
    even when it's not complete or perfect
  - Encourages playing for families and friends
- Fun & laughter – A better environment
  for learning
- Learning strategies and games that work
  best in shared lessons
- Peer support
  - Opportunity to encourage, help,
    and mentor each other
  - Benefit for the one mentored –
    receives help from the mentor
  - Benefit for the mentor –
    learns at a deeper level by teaching someone else
  - Some students get together between lessons and
    play duets and/or help each other
  - Builds relationships while making
    musical progress
  - Teaches students how to play music with others
    (duet or ensemble experience)
  - Provides positive peer pressure –
    "I want to do what he/she is doing!"
- Older students reassured by presence of other
  older students – "I'm not too old"

THE SHARED LESSON ADVANTAGE FOR PARENTS AND STUDENTS

♦ Cheaper than private lessons – 'More bang for your buck'
♦ Opportunity for parents to be part of a group of supportive parents
♦ Opportunity to witness and share in the joy of other's success

THE SHARED LESSON ADVANTAGE FOR TEACHERS

♦ Fun to teach
♦ Less repetitive than private lessons
♦ Higher income potential
♦ Time efficiency for teacher
♦ Ability to make more of an impact – affect more students
♦ Satisfaction levels higher
♦ Happy teacher means happy family and happy students

§§§

My daughter has been learning to play the piano with Simply Music in a shared class for the last five months. At first I was unsure about how the shared class would work, never having experienced them before, but I would now fully recommend them. My daughter has enjoyed making a new friend who also enjoys learning the piano. I feel the shared class has been less intimidating than a one-on-one class and they learn in a collaborative way, each triggering ideas in the other. It has also been helpful for her to listen to how her classmate plays the same piece of music and they learn from each other's mistakes.

Catriona Wells, Parent
Balwyn, Victoria, Australia

CHAPTER 18

COULDN'T GET ENOUGH

A Teen's Piano Passion

By Tami Hays
Riverside, California

Tami Hays has been homeschooled all her life. She is a consummate soccer player, earning various awards, including Most Valuable Person for her high school soccer league. Because of her outstanding efforts, she received an academic and athletic scholarship to California Baptist University.

Limited Song List

Piano: a musical instrument that brings delight and merriment to those listening. In my case, however, those around me were yelling at me to stop playing because I continued to repeat the only few songs that I knew. My playing was driving them crazy. It was obvious that I was passionate about the piano, but I did not enjoy playing as much because of my limited repertoire. I wanted more.

My mom played a huge part in encouraging me to play. Growing up, I have fond memories of her playing every Christmas, just in time for the holiday cheer and Christmas carols. As a musician, she instinctively knew the 'flame' inside of me. At the age of seven, my mom enrolled me in a piano class. Unfortunately, this class only brought tears, grief, and discouragement. I was playing simple, silly songs and could not read a single note. After six months of playing this way, my mom finally relieved me of my torment and tantrums. I quit piano lessons.

A few years later, my mom bought a few video lessons by Simply Music in hopes of resurrecting my love for the piano. I patiently learned new songs, diligently practiced, and thoroughly enjoyed playing. These songs were added to my repertoire. However, it was not enough. My desire to play more songs continued and soon I, and those around me, again grew tired of listening to me play the same songs over and over. For the next few years, I continued to play these songs, but was never satisfied.

Finally, the summer prior to my senior year in high school, my mom asked me if I would like to take piano lessons again. She kept looking for ways to help me play. I think she intuitively knew that she would lose the opportunity for music to be a part of my life if I didn't try again before I went away to college. I was hesitant, but I made sure that she understood that I would only be willing to take lessons if they were from a Simply Music instructor. She knew of a local teacher.

All throughout high school, I never thought about taking a piano class due to my past experience. I was extremely busy keeping up with my heavy homework load and playing soccer for both my club and high school team. I was completely preoccupied with achieving my goals and preparing for college. When my senior year rolled around, I never imagined that I would have time to take piano lessons.

But I did. I enrolled in a Simply Music class. Despite my hectic schedule, I had time to participate, prepare, and practice my songs. Numerous times, my mom demanded I stop playing, otherwise I would have played late into the night.

I was in a class of five. Because the other students were younger and less experienced, I could not move as quickly as I had hoped. However, one day after the group class, my teacher took me aside and asked me if I would like to move forward. She knew, too, how eager I was to learn, so I began private lessons. I 'gobbled up' everything she taught me. This is what I wanted – to release the music inside of me. I was loving piano lessons.

Within a few months, my piano teacher and I took on a huge task in preparation for our upcoming student concert. She wanted to celebrate my senior year by finding a special song to play. My assignment was to find sheet music to any song I desired to learn. After hours of digging through piles of songs at the local piano store, I picked a song – Praise You in the Storm by Casting Crowns. Since I could not read music, my teacher broke the song into comprehensible segments. Despite the difficult sections in the song, I persevered and overcame the challenge. I could play the song from start to finish. What a feat! What an accomplishment! What a joy! At the student concert, I proudly played my practiced piece perfectly. I was so happy.

Recognizing that I was ready, my teacher brought out some Simply Music material that would help me learn to read music. After mastering rhythm, I continued to focus on learning how to read notes. Simply Music takes a different approach to teaching students how to read music. It is more natural, more pleasurable, and more satisfying. I am still in the process of learning how to read music, but I now have a strong foundation to build on. By not forcing students to tackle the painstaking task of reading music at first, Simply Music enables students to enjoy playing the piano from the beginning. At the right age and the right time in a student's instruction, Simply Music appropriately introduces how to read and write music. This way of learning is so much fun and doesn't stifle the pupils' participation and passion to learn more.

Throughout my time learning by the Simply Music method, I have been able to fulfill my inner need to express myself musically. I play the piano with more joy than I had before. Simply Music has heightened my success of learning, playing, and enjoying this musical instrument. Finally! I'm able to bring delight and merriment to those around me, to those who are listening. What a relief.

§§§

I began learning piano with the Simply Music program, motivated by the fact that I could enjoy playing without the boredom of scales and the stress of exams – and come home after each lesson with a new song! Learning to read music in my second year gradually drifted into place and, suddenly, I found I could understand it. I am exactly where I want to be; able to play any piece of music I want and loving every minute of it. All you need to succeed at piano is passion, the Simply Music program, and the love and commitment of a Simply Music teacher.

Jaime-Louise Horton, Student, Age: 17
Perth, Western Australia

CHAPTER 19

BUILDING THE NEXT GENERATION

Music Education for Worship Leaders

By Ernest Amstalden
Jewell, Iowa

A native of Switzerland, Ernest Amstalden was part of a very sought after performance band, recording five albums, the first at the tender age of ten. Ernest is the Senior Pastor of a non-denominational Christian church. In order to train the next generation of worship leaders, he became a Simply Music teacher, opening up a studio which he runs two afternoons and evenings a week to accommodate his forty students.

Worshippers of Old

The Psalmist of old proclaims, "Oh come, let us sing to the Lord! Let us shout joyfully to the Rock of our salvation. Let us come before His presence with thanksgiving; Let us shout joyfully to Him with psalms" (Psalm 95:1-2). It is a well known fact that J.S. Bach, one of the greatest composers of all time, always signed *Soli Deo Gloria* at the end of his compositions, "To the glory of God alone!" And who does not know the song <u>Amazing Grace</u> by John Newton, which has become one of the most beloved and sung worship songs of all times? You probably know the first verse by memory, "Amazing Grace, how sweet the sound that saved a wretch like me. I once was lost but now am found, was blind, but now I see." This song and thousands more have for centuries been sung by people gathering in churches or around the family table to express their thankfulness to God through genuine worship. While some raised their voices to God, others used musical instruments to express their gratitude. We can read in the Bible that King David was a very skilled musician, using the harp, accompanying himself and others, as they were singing joyfully to the Lord their God.

The Needs in the Area of Worship Ministry

Today in churches throughout the world, many different instruments are being used to undergird the singers, worship leaders, and congregations every Sunday. For careful observers, however, there has been a gradual change of 'lead-instruments' being used to accompany the singing. For many years, the organ was the preferred instrument. Then, gradually, the piano came to be the instrument of choice. Today, the trend has been to use guitars, acoustic as well as electric, to do most of the accompanying music. Sometimes churches rely heavily on electric keyboards to accompany the singers.

While there is certainly nothing inherently wrong with all these trends, some years ago I wanted to find out personally why we are witnessing these movements. I went on an investigating journey to find out the real reason of abandoning the piano more and more in our churches. The finding, while not exhaustive or scientific, nevertheless is astounding. Most people I've talked to would love to use the piano to accompany the singers in their church, but all they have to support their ambitions is the Hymn books or some sort of sheet music. Some pianists find it extremely boring playing the same melody the worship leaders or the backup teams are already singing. Their music education consisted of learning to read sheet music and to play only those notes. There is no room for improvisation or even embellishing the songs. And then there is another group of pianists that has never achieved the level of sight-reading necessary to do the job satisfactorily. Instead of looking for other opportunities to enhance their ability to accomplish the task, they succumb to the traditional thinking that 'only the few musically talented ones' can be used in such a setting.

This same principle does not apply when it comes to guitar players. Many great guitarists have never even attempted to use sheet music to play their instruments. Instead, they use the method known as chording to accompany their own singing or to back up some other musicians. They support the melody by playing the chords in a rhythmical fashion that beautifies the song and its lyrics. The play method is simple and does not require complicated musical knowledge. Another factor is the great popularity of contemporary music composed and played by guitarists, that has influenced the younger generation to a great extent. Needless to say, many have picked up a guitar to learn some basic chords and after a short period of time have helped out in churches to support the congregational singing.

The Lack of Training for Accompanists

You probably have heard many statistics on churches in our country. Some of those inform us that over 80% of churches in America have an average attendance of about eighty people on any given Sunday. While these churches are in need of good worship leaders and musicians, very few of them have actually succeeded in this area. It is one of the reasons why many young families have chosen to either travel a great distance to find a large church where they can listen to 'good music' where they can enjoy great worship. Larger churches have a greater pool of musicians to draw from and some hire professionals outright to do the 'music ministry'. If the statistics are correct, most of the 80% of churches in America are in need of worship leaders that have the skill necessary to accompany the congregation with music that is beautifying the worship and glorifying to God.

To accomplish that, you do not have to be a professional musician. There is, however, a great lack of opportunity for aspiring worship leaders in those churches to be properly trained in what we expect them to do. In a traditional environment where piano is being taught, accompaniment training is almost non-existent. Among all those young pianists attending churches every Sunday, an incredible pool of future worship leaders is laying stagnant because of the lack of training for accompanists. Most of them do not even know that there is a teaching method available that would prepare them for this wonderful ministry of leading a worship team.

But there is also skepticism fueled by fear. Personally, I have come across adults who heard some of the students I have trained to lead worship in their respective churches and all they had to say was abundant praise. "That pianist is really something," one said while another came up to me asking, "How is it possible that a boy his age can sing and accompany himself on the piano in such a beautiful way? He truly is an exceptional talent!" The student at that time was eleven-years-old. When I start to explain that if they would be willing to be trained properly, they also would be able to do the same. Their eyes start rolling back into their sockets. "That is impossible! You don't know that I have no musical talents!" You probably have heard similar claims or even have made some of those comments yourself. The bottom line is that there need not be a lack of worship leaders in our churches, no matter what their average weekly attendance is.

To Be a Worship Leader

There are three qualities that you must bring with you to be a candidate to become the next worship leader in your church. You must be willing to forgo the notion that only the talented ones can qualify. You must be willing to embrace a method of learning that is revolutionary and at the same time simple. And the most important quality of all is that a worship leader must have a servant's heart.

For a child who has never played the piano, none of these necessary qualities are threatening. They don't know anything else. Some of them have observed worship leaders and they would love to be able to do the same. Others have never had that privilege and yet they would love to sing and play in their church. It is normally the parents who do not think that their child would be able to accomplish the task. They believe that for their child to become a worship leader, they would have to invest in many years of music lessons and of enduring agonizing sounds of scaling up and down the piano.

And what about adults who already play the piano in church by using the traditional method of reading sheet music? Can they still become an accompanist in their church? The answer is a resounding *Yes!* Any method that is revolutionizing the way you think and do music is a challenge to our status quo. Because the Simply Music method is simple, many people are first skeptical. What the child, as well as the adult, needs is a solid training method that primarily focuses on this unique and very effective style of playing. There are some 'learn in twenty-four hours how to play accompaniment on the piano' methods available. But Simply Music has developed the most comprehensive and yet simple to understand accompaniment program available anywhere. We train our students in generative skills that would allow them to play and sing together, transpose music into different keys, and use variations and sophisticated rhythms that would add to the fullness of the song. These skills can be taught.

The most critical aspect of becoming a worship leader is having a servant's heart. As a pastor, I have probably heard about every excuse why other pastors can't find people who are willing to lead worship in their church. My standard answer is very simple, "Whatever musicians you have in your church, they have not yet learned to serve. Their attitude is self-centered instead of support-centered." Most musicians love to be in the spot light. When I challenge my students to spend more practice time to become more effective in accompanying others, some are quick to respond that they really are not interested in playing 'boring chords'. They want to play solo pieces and become the next Chopin or Mozart. What they are saying has nothing to do with what they learn in the Simply Music program. It has everything to do with their attitude toward real musicianship. I like the man who was explaining to a friend about his days in college. He said, "I never actually was in the top half of my class, but I can say that I was in the group that made the top half possible."

Worship leaders with an attitude of serving others and supporting others are the ones who lead true worship. Worship is not about the soloist, it's about the Lord! The entire worship team brings glory to God and leads others into the presence of God with genuine worship. I had to teach this principle to my entire worship team. Out of seven team members, five are active students in the Simply Music program. They range from the age of ten to fifteen.

My son Peter started playing the digital piano in the worship team when he was nine years of age. First, he was more interested in playing the 'special music' during the offering time. I had to teach him that his attitude would have to change before he could lead others in worship. For a young aspiring boy, this was as hard to swallow as for an accomplished musician. Yet, during the course of two years, he was able to change his attitude from a solo-performer to a serving accompanist. Not long ago, he was able to move up to the grand piano, leading the entire worship team by applying all the contemporary chords, rhythms, and techniques he was able to learn through the Simply Music program. Today, he is more than willing to let someone else play solo-pieces, while he is absolutely in love with supporting and leading the worship team. During that process of attitude change, I also observed another incredible development taking place among his peers. Most of the younger Simply Music students want to become worship leaders just like my son Peter is today. With the right attitude and the right teaching method, the inspiration has no limits. It's like a contagious disease; you cannot stop it from spreading.

Simply Music Hallmark Program in Accompaniment

The primary goal of the Simply Music program as a whole is to achieve unprecedented results. In a very short time period, the student is able to play a huge repertoire by having established a strong foundation of playing. They are being trained in:

♦ Learning to sing as a team
♦ Learning to lose the fear of singing or playing
in front of others
♦ Learning to accompany someone right away
without practicing
♦ Learning to 'stay together' rhythmically
♦ Learning not to be distracted by other participants
♦ Learning to listen to others
♦ Learning by observing others doing their part.

There is no substitute for all these experiences provided by Simply Music. The life lessons are as important as the piano lessons themselves.

It is within the first ten weeks the student is being introduced to the method of accompaniment and is able to easily play songs like <u>Amazing Grace</u>. It is in this environment where all our students are being exposed to the simple chords that can make a song sound so professional. Along the way, as the student has established a strong foundation of playing, he or she will be introduced to the unique Accompaniment Program, which is a part of the comprehensive Simply Music method structure. Every student has been well prepared for this step. What makes this program so unique is the way it is laying a solid foundation first and then building upon this foundation one layer at a time. Once the foundation is laid, which includes all contemporary chords, the ratios and the rhythms are being introduced. This allows every student to get a solid understanding of the basic nature of accompaniment, beginning with the basic chords and eventually ending up with more sophisticated ones. The same is being done with rhythms and embellishments.

Another unique feature of the Simply Music accompaniment program is the ability to identify the chords in any key, which introduces the student to the much needed process of transposing a song into a different key. In today's contemporary worship style, most worship leaders consider the ability to transpose a song an absolute must. It gives them the freedom to *move* within a song that not just embellishes the sound, but also lifts the song to a higher communication level. Those who have been trained and can freely apply this technique today are among the most sought after musicians. The Simply Music program teaches every student to learn this valuable process and to become an expert at it. This is not just important to know as a pianist, but as a worship leader as well.

And there is yet more to come. Simply Music also teaches our students accompaniment variations which allow them to change from a straight rhythm to a swing rhythm, using the same song, the same chords or chord structure they've already learned in the previous program. While it may sound a little bit intimidating at first, most of the students are very familiar with the musical results it creates. Variations of chords, mid-note-runs, and transition runs are commonly used in this setting. And this is exactly what we teach our students in the Simply Music accompaniment variations program. And in many cases, what they have learned is sufficient to accompany most other musicians or singers in a contemporary setting of worship.

Our advanced Simply Music accompaniment program introduces the student to more complicated rhythms, the technique of chord inversions, scale chords, and transposition. Again, some of these musical terms can be intimidating at first, but you will get used to them very quickly as you learn to develop your accompaniment skills to a generative level. It is at this level where everything becomes a lot more personal. The nuances of sounds and rhythms are being determined by the pianist who is now able to put his or her personal "stamp" on the song. Here you learn to create movement, color, and richness that most people can only dream of. It catapults you into another 'accompaniment-world'. You will not just hear the difference, you will be able to *feel* the difference. At this level of playing, you will be well advanced in leading others in worship, using your accompaniment skills you have learned throughout the entire Simply Music program.

And what about singing and playing at the same time? Can that also be learned or must I just have been 'born with that talent'? In our Simply Music program, we call that 'multiple thought-processing'. Once again, that particular challenge is not being taught in a traditional music environment. One of the reasons for this is that most piano lessons are being taught in a private setting, meaning there is only one student being taught at a time. In the Simply Music method, we are addressing this issue head on right from the beginning – the very first lesson. We teach our method in a class environment, meaning that multiple students are learning the same piano technique at the same time. This gives the teacher the opportunity to introduce a new song where one of the students learns the accompaniment structure of the song while the rest supplies the melody by singing the song. A rotation during the lesson allows for the students to be a part of both experiences.

A Final Word of Encouragement

If you are a pastor or a church board member, let me encourage you to take a very close look at what is going on in your local church regarding worship. Take an active part in providing an environment where your next generation can be motivated to be properly trained and nurtured to become a part of your worship team. Young people need guidance and training. The guidance will have to be provided by those in spiritual and parental leadership, while the training can be delegated to a well-trained Simply Music instructor. With this guidance and training, they can lead the church community with passion to say, "Come, let us worship and bow down, let us kneel before the Lord our Maker" (Psalm 95:6). Remember, the possibilities are endless and with God nothing is impossible.

§§§

I believe that there is a void in the music world today of keyboardists who have developed the skills of accompaniment. Simply Music simplifies the process to learn and master this much needed skill, by teaching the students to see chords as simple 'shapes' and to play them in a way that is not complicated. This allows them to develop freedom of expression in their playing ability and experience how fun it can be to accompany other musicians and singers! Using the tools of accompaniment that Simply Music teaches, even young children can develop this skill that will give them the ability to experience what I call 'playing music in the real world'.

Ray Nelson, Simply Music Teacher, Former YWAM (Youth with a Mission) Staff Member, Music Team Trainer/Developer for the School of Worship at the University of the Nations
Cambridge, New Zealand

CHAPTER 20

TEACHERS IN COOPERATION

Building a Support System for Success

By Laurie Richards
Omaha, Nebraska

Laurie Richards is a classically trained pianist. She has taught the Simply Music method for seven years and has a growing piano studio of over seventy-five students. Laurie and her husband Mike homeschool their three children and are actively involved in their church. The entire family is learning to play piano the Simply Music way. Their oldest son has Downs Syndrome and they are advocates for those with special abilities.

Goodwill

My last memory before losing consciousness was of looking out and seeing a giant blue semi-truck right outside my car window immediately before the impact. A few weeks later the truck driver would tell my husband that he would never, ever be able to get the look on my face out of his mind.

I was the front passenger in a van and the semi – carrying 76,000 pounds of cargo – was able to slow down only to forty-five mph before striking the van. I woke up a short while later before the 'jaws of life' had arrived to get most of the six passengers out. A man who had stopped to help was sitting with me. I heard him say to someone, "It looks like she took the brunt of it," and I knew he was talking about me. I knew what had happened and that I was badly injured, but at that time had no idea to what extent or if I would even survive. I was life-flighted to the hospital where it was determined I had ten broken bones from my back all the way down to my left foot, nerve damage, and several other minor injuries.

I spent three weeks in the hospital then continued recovering at home in a hospital bed, surrounded by hospital equipment and donning various contraptions to aid the healing. About one month after the accident I was able to start walking again, with the aid of first a walker, then crutches, then a cane, and eventually unaided once again.

My Simply Music studio had recently experienced a growth spurt and I had around fifty students. My studio was my family's main source of income, but now my business had unexpectedly come to a screeching halt. At that time there were three other Simply Music teachers in my area – Janita Pavelka, Anne Smith, and Michele Favero-Kluge. What they did for me and my family was extraordinarily generous; it is something almost unheard of in our competitive culture. Between the three of them, they arranged to teach every one of my classes, every week at my home studio, asking for absolutely nothing in return. They taught my classes for two full months, while maintaining their own piano studios and their own lives. They did it so that I would still have an income while I was recovering and so my business wouldn't suffer. People like this, who share so unselfishly, are an inspiration. I will always be grateful for their love and friendship.

It may seem natural to view a nearby piano teacher as a competitor, someone in a position to *take* new students away from you, affecting your business. This, unfortunately, seems to be the typical mindset. But, my story illustrates how beneficial it can be to form a cooperative association amongst piano teachers seeking to strengthen and help one another. There truly is strength in numbers. While I was the recipient of the most obvious benefit in my story, everyone involved comes out ahead in the long run. Goodwill always comes back to the giver in some form.

A Contagious Vision

Culturally, we have a perception of what piano lessons look like. A huge number of adults have either taken piano lessons as children and quit out of frustration or boredom, or know someone who has had that type of experience. They attach negative emotions to piano lessons. They may assume that any piano lessons would result in a similar experience. But what if you, as a piano teacher, offered something with passion and conviction that was truly unique and different? What if you provided immediate results, no matter what one's experience and background? What if you have a program so remarkable that it excluded absolutely no one from the promise that he or she could be musically self-expressed? What if you could help people fulfill lifelong dreams and change lives, young and old?

The obvious answer is that you would want to communicate these opportunities to as many people as possible. A good problem to have is that you probably would have more piano students than you could handle alone. This can be a typical scenario when offering Simply Music piano lessons especially with a cooperative team effort mindset.

When I became a licensed Simply Music teacher, Janita Pavelka was the only other teacher in my area. I called her to ask about the Simply Music program. We connected immediately and became good friends as well as colleagues. We lived about twenty miles apart and served different areas of our city. Once I got my studio up and running, she and I began meeting monthly to share teaching ideas, brainstorm marketing plans, and pool what funds we could to grow our studios. We met together with a local marketing consultant for new ideas and helped each other follow through on them. Without her support and her brainstorming, there is no doubt in my mind that I could not have been nearly as successful as I have been.

For a few years, Janita and I were the only teachers in our area. With some creative marketing we were each able to enjoy growing businesses as well as a deepening passion for the Simply Music curriculum and mission. When she initially began recommending that we recruit new teachers, my knee-jerk response was one of uncertainty. But Simply Music teachers can't be selfish about this program. It has too much to offer. One of the tag lines of the company is "A world where everyone plays". This isn't an advertising gimmick; it actually is the vision of Neil Moore, the founder of Simply Music. It occurred to me that our society needs a vision like this and it needs people who are dedicated to working toward this vision. Think of the impact it could have on our culture if every person were able to express himself musically. If Simply Music teachers really believe in this vision and if we agree that we need it to be taken seriously, then we can help make it happen, but not by fending for ourselves and marking our territories with invisible boundary lines. I am excited about moving in the direction of "a world where everyone plays". By uniting as a teacher body

175

and working cooperatively, we can give as many people as possible access to Simply Music. It's wonderful to have a network of local teachers who are just as excited about it as I am.

Benefits of a Cooperative Teacher Association

There are many professional, emotional, and financial benefits of working alongside and supporting other teachers. Simply Music piano lessons themselves are most successful in a shared lesson format. We can apply some of the same 'shared lesson' philosophy to cooperative teacher groups.

Community/Camaraderie. So many things in life are just more enjoyable when shared. Simply Music is non-traditional, so there may be people who don't understand the approach and reject it because of the lack of understanding. That's why it's great to have like-minded teachers to talk with regularly who share your understanding of and passion for this method. Positive feedback and interaction always provide an attitude boost. Janita shared this story: A student's parent came to a lesson and commented, "I saw your competitor's sign the other day." "My competitor?" she asked. She couldn't figure out who this competitor could be. It turned out to be the nearest Simply Music teacher, a friend and colleague whom Janita had helped get started in Simply Music. Two things stood out to me; that the parent had assumed two teachers of the same method were competitors and that the same thought had never even occurred to Janita. It is a testament to her pure motives and mindset regarding her Simply Music business.

Studio growth. Having colleagues nearby can increase your student base, not decrease it. By virtue of all the extra relationship connections that wouldn't otherwise exist, Simply Music teachers help spread the word to more people, which *increases* the opportunity to grow your business. When my teacher friends temporarily taught my classes, they made a lot of new contacts for themselves. With my students being taught by different teachers, they and their parents were able to relate their experiences with those teachers directly to their friends, family, and colleagues. They also saw first-hand, the caliber of teachers in our area who teach Simply Music and they appreciated their sacrifice of time, energy, and finances on my behalf.

Sharing a variety of strengths. We can always gain something from other people's experience and perspective. Most of us excel in one area or another or have more natural ability in a particular area. Here are a few examples of strengths that different members of our current group of Omaha teachers have:

- ◆ Detail-Oriented – help teachers learn efficient administrative tasks, share ideas for keeping track of student and lesson details; share useful forms they have developed, take minutes at meetings to be shared with the entire group.

- ◆ Big Picture Thinker – keep the Simply Music vision in the forefront as we discuss and develop the day-to-day strategies of running our studios.

- ◆ Public Relations – research and share opportunities for educating our communities about Simply Music. On my own, I could not have come up with a fraction of the ideas that other members have shared. My studio has benefited immensely from these ideas.

- ◆ Financial Background – budgeting, balancing, and reporting activity in the teacher association's bank account; tax return tips, serving as treasurer for the group.

- ◆ Organizer – help plan the meetings and create agendas; plan and prepare for publicity events and regional training.

The list could go on. But these are just a few examples of the strengths present in our group that have helped each of us maintain a well-rounded and balanced perspective as well as successful individual studios. As the saying goes "iron sharpens iron".

Teamwork. Janita and I once co-taught a Simply Music class at a local Homeschool Learning Center. At the first session, we both conducted the Foundation Session by taking turns with the different sections and commenting where appropriate during the other's sections. She and I both had similar comments afterward, "I really liked how you presented that particular section", or "That was a great visual to use", or "I hadn't thought to use that particular example before. That was really helpful". It helped both of us to improve our own techniques. There were around twelve children enrolled so we divided the class into two; I taught the younger ones and Janita taught the teenagers. We only had one room to use. We each brought our own keyboards and took our classes to opposite ends of the room. It actually was fun to have another group in the same room and occasionally one group would share something with the other. This entire experience was beneficial to everyone involved and it was fun! Several of those students came to our private studios and have continued for several years.

Sharing expenses. Sharing advertising expenses is an obvious benefit of coming together. Advertising is expensive. With several teachers contributing, you can budget advertising funds to support ads that are larger, are longer running, reach more people, or are a combination of these. This is just common business sense. You spend less than you would on singular marketing, but you have greater reach. With the larger group you have more buying power.

Ongoing support and training. Everyone in our teacher group appreciates the close proximity of teachers willing to help and support one another. Although there are many support systems in place for all Simply Music teachers, sometimes a phone call to a nearby colleague and friend is the most effective support. We have the option of getting together as often as we want with a piano available for training if needed.

As our teacher body has grown, we have tried to include a training component in most meetings and occasionally hold training-only sessions. We may *teach* each other a song in order to demonstrate certain teaching techniques. At one training meeting, everyone was asked to come with an original composition to share. This was uncomfortable for some; however, it is a vital step toward being an effective coach in the composition area. Teachers with more experience are available to help support newer teachers. We are a friendly group, so teachers don't feel intimidated.

Nuts and Bolts of a United Teacher Body

What does a cooperative teacher body look like? Here are several ways the Omaha Simply Music teachers have come together as a cooperative association.

Holding regular meetings. All teachers in the area are invited to come together and share ideas regarding marketing, teaching the Simply Music curriculum, resolving issues within their studios, planning events, and any number of related topics. Along with the support and training mentioned before, here are a few other things we have done at our meetings:

♦ Share resources, such as music for the accompaniment and reading programs
♦ Plan and discuss the content of our shared website
♦ Share successes and challenges.

It is a time of fellowship, food, and fun while enjoying the company of others who 'carry the same flag'.

When we know someone is going to start the Simply Music teacher training program, our group invites them to the very next meeting. Here is what one brand new teacher trainee said after attending her first meeting:

What a great bunch! I haven't even received my teacher training packet, but I already get the feeling that I was destined for Simply Music! Wow! Just the mindset and the pure love of music. I love the forward-thinking mentality, and I love that each teacher seems to bring different strengths to the table. Thank you for welcoming me so readily. I am just ecstatic about this whole thing!

She knows that she has a strong support system already in place and close by. What a great way to start your new business!

Pooling resources. As our teacher body has grown, we have mutually decided to form a local Simply Music Teacher Association and open a bank account in the same name. Each member contributes an agreed upon amount every month. One teacher agreed to handle the collecting and depositing of money. The funds are used to pay for marketing and advertising expenses which benefit the entire area, such as the yellow pages ad, dues for business networking groups, trade show expenses, and area-wide ads. These funds are also used to pay for brochures which list all of the teachers' names, area of town, and contact information. These brochures are used at publicity events.

Substituting for one another. On occasion when a teacher has a scheduling conflict with classes, she may call on another teacher in the area to teach those classes rather than canceling or rescheduling them. The teacher is paid a set amount for her time.

Community teaching and referring. Often teachers take advantage of community teaching opportunities to help people find out about Simply Music. Some examples are offering workshops through:

♦ Homeschool learning center
♦ A community-wide arts program offering low-cost art and music classes
♦ College for Kids summer classes offered through a local community college.

Teachers who offer these classes are paid by the organization. The teachers typically make quite a bit less for these workshop classes than they do in their private studios. When the workshop class is completed, students must enroll in a private studio in order to continue with Simply Music. The teacher will refer students to the teachers who are closest to them geographically. Janita helped a new teacher get his studio started this way. She offered a College for Kids class in his suburb and most of the students she taught continued in his new studio.

Being available for support. Support offered in smaller doses and on a regular basis is just as important. This happens at our regular meetings, but also outside of scheduled get-togethers. This is especially helpful for newly licensed teachers who know that support is a phone call away and close to home. Often they are only looking for encouragement as they prepare for their very first Free Introductory Session or class. A little encouragement goes a long way when venturing into new territory. Often newer teachers will sit in on other teachers' Free Introductory Sessions or classes to help them get started on their own.

Combining for larger events. Some teachers have large studios. Others prefer to keep theirs' small. The larger studios will often invite another teacher's studio to join them for recitals or events. This gives the students in the smaller studio the opportunity to experience a more public venue for sharing their musical talents.

Sharing studio space and new students. Recently, I moved my studio from my home to a commercial space in a shopping center. Shortly after the move, two of my studio parents decided to go through the teacher training program and began teaching Simply Music. I was teaching about fifteen hours over four days per week so the studio was vacant much of the time. Since I didn't want to expand my hours and was still getting regular calls about Simply Music, the timing was ideal to offer my studio for rent to the new teachers. We decided to take turns conducting the Free Introductory Sessions about Simply Music, but would offer *all* of the class times that were available between the three of us to prospective students, rather than working separately to fill up classes. This worked out well. Through our cooperative efforts both teachers were able to start classes almost immediately upon being licensed, with ten to fifteen students each in their first few months.

Staffing booths for publicity. We try to consistently get the Simply Music name out in public by buying booths at home school conventions, teacher conventions, educational resource fairs, trade shows, and other venues. The teachers take turns staffing these events and sharing all the teachers' contact information so that a nearby teacher can be located for prospective students. We bring drawing slips for visitors to register for a free month of piano lessons. After the event, the slips are divided among the teachers who are nearest to the address on the drawing slip. Each teacher offers as many free months as they would like in order to attract new students.

There are so many different ways to support one another in our business endeavors. I believe that each and every effort by the involved teachers strengthens our individual businesses in the long run and often immediately, as well.

A Marketing Mindset

A cooperative teacher association requires individual. teachers to adopt more of a 'big picture' mindset. Think of your entire area as being filled with hundreds, thousands, or even hundreds-of-thousands of people who need to hear about all the benefits of Simply Music. Could you possibly accommodate this many students or even prospective students? Unless you live in a very isolated location, chances are you need to enlist other teachers to help you spread the word and then absorb the response. You automatically benefit from having a nearby colleague who shares your passion.

Think about your circle of influence – all those people you know, in every area of your life, who could possibly be influenced by you in some way. You may have influence based on your knowledge in some area, your personality, skills, a particular talent, or any number of other reasons. If you are a musician and someone asks you if you know of a good piano teacher, that person is in your circle of influence even if you do not know them. So, your circle of influence directly impacts your business.

Now consider the circle of influence of each of your piano students and parents. Since your students experience success in their lessons, you will likely attract new students from their circle, and on, and on. If you have another teacher in your area, she and her students have their own circles. Your circle of influence is not limited to your own neighborhood or zipcode. The more teachers and students you have, the greater the potential impact. A person across town may have heard about Simply Music from a friend, who heard from a co-worker whose son took Simply Music piano lessons. This person looks for a teacher closer to her own house. It's easy to see how this grows exponentially and benefits everyone as more and more people become familiar with Simply Music.

At a networking seminar I attended, the speaker had some unusual, but very wise advice regarding networking. At networking events, he said, don't look at all the people in the room and see twenty prospective clients. Rather, view them as twenty potential referral sources. Each of those twenty people has their own set of family, friends, coworkers, acquaintances, etc. Go up to them and ask about *their* businesses. Ask how you can help *them*. Above all, be genuine. They will remember you. When people in their circle of influence ask if they know of a piano teacher, you want them to think of you because you were friendly, genuine, and helpful. His philosophy is that the goodwill you share, with pure motives, always returns to you in some form. I think of this philosophy as a foundation of our Omaha group.

Here is a definition of the word cooperative: "involving mutual assistance in working toward a common goal; willing to be of assistance". I like the different pieces of this definition and how it relates to our teacher group.

- ♦ Mutual Assistance – the give-and-take nature of working together; you help and support others, they help and support you, everyone benefits.

184

- ♦ Common Goal – It's so fulfilling to have others who are working toward the same goal and who understand your passion; long-lasting friendships are usually the result.
- ♦ Willing – teachers must have pure intentions in a cooperative group. They must truly want to help their colleagues succeed and have the will to work together.

We can help each other reach our goals as Simply Music teachers, as a unified body with genuine caring and support of one another and with combined resources to reach more people. How grateful I am that I benefited from this when that semi-truck hit my van.

§§§

I have learned that being a Simply Music teacher is about so much more than just piano. I have gained insights about life, relationships, and parenting that I would never have imagined from a piano program. The Simply Music community is one of the most supportive I have ever found. In fact, I recently moved across the country and my best friend and strongest support in my new community is another Simply Music teacher whom I would never have known otherwise. We market together, teach together, and encourage each other to expand our businesses, music, and ourselves in ways we might never have done alone.

Kathy Kiger, Simply Music Teacher
Frisco, Texas

CHAPTER 21

PURSUING A SECOND CAREER

Living Out Your Passions

By Gordon Harvey
Malvern East, Victoria, Australia

Gordon Harvey began piano lessons at the age of thirty-five and has been teaching the Simply Music method for fifteen years. He built a series of teaching studios while establishing the Australian Simply Music business with a colleague. He is now the National Manager of Simply Music, Australia. As a Senior Teacher Trainer, he creates/develops programs and online content that assist teachers around the world.

A Change of Course

I'd worked in the book industry for many years, mostly as a sales rep with a major publisher. Although it was an enjoyable enough career, I didn't feel satisfied or fulfilled. I wanted those working hours of each day to be spent doing something that reflected my passions. One of the true constants in my life was music. I had been a performing musician and composer in the field of ambient and electronic music. I wasn't inspired by the struggle of trying to make a living as a musician, though, especially in my obscure field. I also was looking for a path that allowed me to make an income while still having time to develop myself musically.

I met Neil Moore just at the time when he was making a similar life change. He'd decided to dedicate himself to music and soon found an opportunity for teaching. I was very impressed with Neil as a person. His single-minded commitment to his chosen path led me to think that anything he took on deserved being taken seriously. At the very least, for the first time, I could dip my toe into the waters of playing piano which would clearly enhance my musical skills. But very quickly I began to imagine myself working as a teacher.

I was thrilled by the prospect of combining a career with a passion. The idea was that I would teach part-time and devote the rest of my time to writing music. Although many of our teachers are doing just that, it's not how it worked out for me! I discovered a love of teaching – the experience of my students developing and finding musical self-expression was as rewarding as doing the same for myself. Before I knew it, teaching had become full-time.

As an adult beginner on piano rather than a seasoned performer like most piano teachers, I was nervous that my students would see right through me, pretending to be a 'real teacher'. As it turned out, it wasn't like that at all. I really did have something to offer beginning students. So long as I was prepared and trained in the detail of presenting the pieces, the lessons unfolded successfully. I'm always forthright about my experience, saying that my only real qualification is being a fully trained and accredited teacher of the Simply Music method. To the best of my knowledge I've never had a student concerned about my lack of traditional qualifications. Over the years, I've needed to keep myself trained ahead of my students and focus on the Simply Music syllabus pieces in my practice. Fortunately, the pieces I was learning were fun in themselves!

Of course, it wasn't pure pleasure. There was no guarantee of success and certainly no guarantee of a regular income. I had to build from nothing. I expected it to take a while before I was earning the amount I did in my previous job. I knew there wouldn't be the same reliable income each month. I was fortunate that, unlike most small businesses, teaching required minimal startup costs. I'd waited until I qualified for an employment bonus before I left my job. That was enough to launch my business without having to secure additional finance. I very quickly learned to appreciate a difference in being self-employed. My efforts are reflected in my earnings – the fruits of every success go to me, not my employer. And I learned a lot about responsibility by experiencing the fruits of my failures!

A New Approach to a Career

There are many aspects of a teaching career with Simply Music which make it uniquely suitable for a mature person looking for a change; a retiree, a professional who is looking at his life and rethinking his priorities, or perhaps a mom with grown up kids who is wanting to reintroduce herself to the workforce. Few other businesses allow you to be so entrepreneurial choosing where you work, when you work, and with whom you work. Most of our teachers work from home, but those who choose can build a bigger business which is much more profitable.

There is no special equipment needed other than your piano. Teachers have tremendous flexibility. Some teachers elect to teach only adult students, or only children, only shared lessons or only private, only daytime or only evening classes.

For someone like me, or anyone who hasn't gone through formal training in education, Simply Music is an opportunity you couldn't get elsewhere. There are many traditional teachers who are very much on their own, picking up books, looking out for new ideas, trying out different things with their students, in the hope of sifting through what's available until they find a blend that works for them. By comparison, Simply Music is very structured, following a carefully designed Teacher Training program that has been proven to work. It is unfolded in a clear, step-by-step fashion. The materials are comprehensive and easy to use. The resources, as well as the interaction and support from the worldwide family of other Simply Music teachers, assist with just about every curriculum question imaginable. While there's plenty of work involved with learning to teach a huge number of pieces and styles, the experience of teaching Simply Music is a lot like the experience of our students. Put simply, you stick carefully to the program and you succeed.

While you're ultimately responsible for your own success, you're not left on your own in a business sense. Simply Music provides a range of professionally produced marketing materials, which a fully independent teacher couldn't dream of emulating. Again, a wealth of training, coaching and advice are available from both the organization and the community of hundreds of other teachers on customer relations and running a business.

Tommy Toy, from Mill Valley, California, gave up a successful corporate career to satisfy a thirty year passion for sharing music. Here's how he describes the experience:

When I first told my friends, family, and colleagues that I was resigning my position as a senior advertising executive, changing careers and essentially becoming a piano teacher, I vividly remember a comment from one of my less tactful clients, which I think was on everyone's mind: "You'll be a great 'riches-to-rags' tale."

Though they wished me well, most could not understand how I could leave a successful fifteen year professional career to become a piano teacher, typically one of the lowest paid professions with terrible reputations as taskmaster ogres.

In reality, if it were not for Simply Music, I would never have made the move. Simply Music made it easy to be successful at being a piano teacher – financially, professionally, educationally, and spiritually.

Simply Music provides comprehensive, easy-to-execute curriculum; amazingly thorough, consistent training materials, sound, logical business philosophy – all the tools needed to build a thriving successful small business that is rewarding to run.

If it were not for Simply Music, I'd probably still be trying to convince the world we need more laundry detergent, instead of needing more music. I'd like to think my Simply Music experience has been more of a great 'riches-to-riches' tale. Thank you Simply Music for opening the doors to change my life!

Many teachers have said that they've experienced health and well-being benefits. There's something about music that makes it feel like a privilege to be part of. And many of us deeply appreciate the chance to give something back by sharing what we know. In the sharing, we gain even more for ourselves.

For me, being part of Simply Music has been a personal growth experience, which has affected my life far beyond just teaching people to play. So much about a successful outcome to piano teaching has to do with powerful and clear communication, knowing how we most effectively learn, and understanding the dynamics of relationships. The Simply Music approach is built on these fundamentals and the training is unique in the way it coaches teachers to be the best individuals they can possibly be.

The Adult Student

As an instructor, it is easy to become very attached to your students. Watching them grow musically, seeing each one uncover music's particular expression in their life, is deeply rewarding and uniquely revealing. But with adult students, there is an additional layer of meaning. For many of them, music has been a life time dream that for one reason or another has remained unfulfilled. There's a story behind every adult who comes to you – perhaps they had an unsympathetic music teacher at school who suppressed, but could never quite extinguish the flame. Perhaps, they were never given the opportunity to learn. I had a student who had childhood lessons. In her classes with me, she had the habit of pulling her hands away quickly from the keyboard whenever she made a mistake. When I asked her about this, she explained that her teacher at school would rap her knuckles with the edge of a ruler. And yet she came back to lessons years later.

Music accompanies people through their life's experiences into adulthood and beyond. And they identify themselves with particular songs or styles; it can become a companion with which they develop a deeply personal relationship. As their appreciation of music matures and the gap widens in their perception between themselves and those who make music, they still hold on to the possibility of closing that gap, perhaps waiting until they quit their job or until the children have left home.

Growing numbers of retirees are becoming Simply Music students. Many of them are taking up an endeavor widely known to help maintain healthy brain activity. They are also fulfilling a long-held dream of creative expression. The longer the dream is cocooned, the more profound the experience of finally realizing it. I've had many students moved to tears by the simple experience of hearing real music flowing through their fingers. One of my students in her sixties took up music as a way of rebuilding her life after her husband died. She gave herself the challenge of learning her husband's favorite song, which she felt guided her through the grieving process. Although it was a sometimes tearful project, when it was completed she told me she felt a sense of liberation. And at the same time she had found a small way to remember and honor her husband.

At least 35% of our students are aged twenty and over, with more than half of these over fifty. This is a fast-growing segment of our market, as the population ages and people spend a greater proportion of their lives in retirement. Thanks to the flexibility of the Simply Music business model, many of our teachers can fit their choice of a part-time occupation by teaching adult students. Some teachers specifically target adult students, advertising in publications for retirees, teaching from retirement villages. Retirees can typically be taught during the day, giving teachers the opportunity to work while their children are at school and avoiding the usual after-school and weekend teaching regimes.

Mature-age Career Change

For those older people with some existing musical background, the same growth experience can be found in teaching. If you've been fortunate enough to have music as part of your life for a long time, there's often a desire to 'give something back'. The consistent view for people is that music is one of the top five most important parts of their lives. It means a lot to many retirees to be able to pass on their experience. And, like me, the idea of making an income doing something you love is cause for a rethinking of their priorities.

For a senior person, a career change is perhaps a more daunting prospect than it is for others. There needs to be a sense of 'letting go' – a willingness to accept fresh perspectives on what may be life time habits and assumptions. Piano teachers who choose the Simply Music method may have switched from successful businesses presenting more traditional methods and have had to set aside practices they have employed for years. This can also apply to those who've played all their lives, but have never taught. There can be the layers of personal meaning they've attached to music over the years, which may or may not be relevant to the whole new experience of teaching. Sometimes our biggest fear is of what's unknown.

Joanne Jones, from Riverton, West Australia, is one who faced her fears and moved into teaching from a long-term professional career. At age sixty-four, this is her story:

In spite of a high level of piano experience, playing seriously since the age of eight, and moving on to working as an accompanist for soloists, choirs, and musicals, I was painfully aware of the fact that I didn't actually understand what I was playing. I could read and play quite competently, but without the written instruction I was totally stymied. I had never connected the theory to the actual playing.

After acknowledging the fact that few people end up being able to play the piano after childhood lessons, I decided that the 'traditional' approach to piano instruction was profoundly lacking somewhere in its delivery. I felt utter frustration personally, as music was definitely a part of my identity and yet it did not allow me to express myself beyond interpreting someone else's music. There was no sense of freedom with this 'something' that I felt was an intrinsic part of me.

I began a thirty year search for an alternative way of learning piano. Every 'new' way I researched ended up being another reading-based approach with the same basic weakness. I had all but stopped playing by the time Simply Music entered my life. We had been living overseas for ten years and on return to Australia I had become a Real Estate Consultant, which took all my time and energy for the following ten years. Playing piano had taken a back seat, to the point that I had to admit that I was on the brink of being someone who used to play the piano, an unthinkable state for someone whose identity rested so much in that arena. The thought of restoring my pieces the 'old' way filled me with dread hours of scales to restore my strength and hours of study to restore the pieces, many of which held no allure for me at all.

My wonderful mum, who had made sure that we all learned an instrument and used our talents beyond the home, had been gravely ill for some years. So I took time out to be with her before she died. This break enabled me to extricate myself from real estate and be open to a whole new direction. While searching, I came across Simply Music. I hoped, beyond hope, that finally I may have found a way back into my music that would lead to playing with freedom at last! Quite understandably I was very skeptical at first, but I began lessons and was determined to follow instructions to the letter and finally unlock the mystery of the keyboard.

As I write this, tears of gratitude well up at the thought of what this program has given me, how it has transformed my musical experience and given me a whole new joyous career when others my age are thinking of retiring.

To my utter relief and delight I had found a program that actually DELIVERED ON ITS PROMISE – a breakthrough at last! My only concern was that there were no specific exercises set to strengthen my fingers. I was traditional to the core! But to my amazement and, again, relief, my fingers have strengthened simply by playing the pieces as have those of my students.

Simply Music has given me back the gift of playing far beyond any level of expertise that I had before. In a practical sense, Simply Music does not allow me to sail blithely on without understanding what is happening beneath my hands. Using simple pieces to both teach and apply a basic set of tools brings an awareness of the patterns and shapes that music creates on the piano. This has given me access to a way of playing songs that has become a vehicle, taking me to otherwise inaccessible musical places. In this process, a knowing begins to grow that blossom into far more than the sum of its parts as I become more and more familiar with them, developing the understanding of the theory by playing. How wonderful is that?

I also believe Simply Music has begun to unblock my own creativity. The tools given to me by Simply Music have actually opened my mind to how I operate in my daily life, to become aware of things that I didn't know I wasn't aware of!

It would be a huge oversight for me not to say just how valuable the opportunity to teach Simply Music has been in my own development as a player. The wise saying that 'by our pupils we are taught' could not be more succinctly demonstrated than in the case of teaching this program. Every single day I am being reminded of where I need to be focused my self, as well as seeing more and more exactly what is unfolding on the keyboard beneath my hands and those of my pupils. I could never be bored, or more excited about the musical possibilities both of my students and myself, AND I am being paid to do it, which means I can be at the keyboard for many more hours than would otherwise be possible!

The ability to choose our hours and place of work, to work with others who love music, and to spread the message of the fundamental musical nature of human beings are great reasons to become a Simply Music teacher, especially for the retiree. It is also an honor to be a part of Simply Music for which we will always be grateful. For those of us whom music is a natural, essential, everyday part of life regardless of how we made a living, the bonus of earning an income from our passion is a genuine privilege.

§§§

Although my career as a chiropractor had its rewards, the yearning for musical expression in my life was constant. After closing my practice, earning a B.A. in music, and still not at ease at the piano, I almost accepted that I would 'never have what it takes' to be a musician. Then I discovered the Simply Music program and found that I could easily and immediately express myself musically. I made a new career for myself by helping others of all ages to do the same thing.

Victoria Shirley, Simply Music Teacher
Herald, California

CHAPTER 22

1-2-3 BLASTOFF

Getting My Piano Business Off to a Great Start

By Bethany McBride
Colstrip, Montana

Bethany McBride is twenty-three-years-old. She grew up in a very musical family. Bethany attended a private high school that emphasized music and the fine arts including all-state choirs, orchestras, small and large group ensembles, contest solos, and duets. Currently, she leads the worship team at her church with keyboard and vocals. In the first five months of business, she built a studio with twenty-eight new students. Simply Music is her first entrepreneurial endeavor.

Enthusiasm

Young adults are known to be energetic, unreserved, and determined. I'm no different! When it came to finding a business opportunity that would bring success quickly, I wanted it *now*. I also longed for a job that would make an impact in people's lives to do something meaningful – a job that I could love that would produce a sustainable income for my family. I wanted more. Pleasantly surprised, I got everything I wanted and I got it fast.

I discovered Simply Music on the internet and realized that this would be an awesome business opportunity. It was a business I could do from my home; I could invest in people's lives. And most importantly, it was something I could see myself doing for years to come. I immersed myself whole-heartedly into this business endeavor. At first, I set my goals fairly low because I didn't know what kind of results to expect in a small rural area. I planned for five students from my first Free Introductory Session.

I began thinking of ways to recruit potential students. I was working at an after-school program where children were able to come and get help on homework. I began talking about Simply Music with parents. Everywhere I went, I talked about Simply Music; the grocery store, restaurants, and even when bumping into people on the sidewalk. I began to save their contact information so that I could follow up as I scheduled my first Free Introductory Session. I called and emailed more than sixty potential students and their parents. Ten families showed up and eight students began lessons. That absolutely thrilled me!

I called all the rest of the families who had expressed interest and informed them about the second Free Introductory Session. Two families came to this session and three more students started. Eleven students within my first two weeks! I didn't feel comfortable at first contacting people more than one time, but realized that some people need to be encouraged. After calling potential students from my contact list again, I began my first lessons with seventeen students. I was absolutely stunned, scared, thrilled, excited, and nervous, all in one!

A vital part of my success for my studio has been my openness and honesty about myself, my expectations for my studio, and my lack of experience as a teacher (I did not have any previous teaching experience). I spoke from my heart about Simply Music. They sensed that I was being sincere and passionate, not trying to sell them something.

A Little Background

I took traditional piano lessons from kindergarten to eighth grade. I could play by ear very well. I learned to play what I heard and what sounded good, not necessarily what was written on the page. Playing from the page limited me tremendously. Also, it never made sense to me to play all those repeated scales and drills. Bless my mother's heart! For those nine years, she practically had to pull my teeth (and pull her own hair) just to get me to practice. Without my mother's persistence, I would not be able to play the piano today.

I grew up in a very musical family, but I hated piano. It was boring. I never felt comfortable expressing myself; it felt limiting. It was as if I was stuck in a little box kicking and screaming for someone to open it up so that my creativity and gifts could pop out and yell, "surprise!" When I listened to bands that had keyboards, I often wondered how many years they had been taking lessons to get where they were. If nine years of lessons resulted in child-like playing, they must have taken lessons for centuries! Simply Music has taught me more in the last five months than in nine years of traditional lessons. In a short amount of time, it has opened up doors in my personal ability to play piano in more ways than I can describe. It gave me the key to unlock what had been hiding inside of me for years and years. 'Pop-goes-the-weasel' musical expression is revealed. What a blast!

Stories like mine kept surfacing in the studio. Students who had studied traditionally for years were learning to play quickly and easily through Simply Music. At first it was a surprise to me, but I found out that these stories reflect a common experience. Simply Music is worth more than what you pay for it!

Growing My Business

With my personal growth came a fulfilling and lucrative business. I continue to find ways to increase my student numbers. I often ask people where they have heard about Simply Music and it is usually from word of mouth. I use flyers, word of mouth, word of mouth some more, and word of mouth again. When I take a look at my entire body of students, 90% of them have heard about Simply Music from me personally. I try not to let a day go by without talking about Simply Music. I live in a small town in Eastern Montana, and let me tell you, word of mouth carries very fast. I cannot say this enough! Word of mouth is the biggest asset to gaining students.

For instance, referrals. I give my students credit for a month of lessons for every referred student who enrolls with my studio. They are giving me students that I probably wouldn't have otherwise and I in turn thank them by giving a free month's tuition for the new recruit. I also let people know that if they are not satisfied after the first month's lessons that I will reimburse them 100%.

Communication is key. Emails, monthly newsletters, my webpage, and social networking are an easy way to educate my students and parents about Simply Music. I encourage them with tidbits of fun information, practice techniques, and student concerts. This in turn keeps families excited about Simply Music. They are happy to refer others to me.

Public performances are another facet to building a studio. These help students build their confidence and give them playing experience. Students also learn from other students' performances. These events also give family members an opportunity to see how far students have come in a short amount of time. This helps them to encourage and support their students. It also provides the public an opportunity to see what Simply Music is about.

Some ways of advertising cost little to no money. Community events are one avenue to do this. I can't stress enough how much this involvement in the community has grown my studio. For our Fourth of July event, I set up a booth and had a drawing for a free month's lesson. Ten people registered for the drawing, resulting in three new students. That was a pretty *great* investment considering the booth only cost me $25.00 in fees!

Business networking is also very valuable in building my business. Recently, I joined the Chamber of Commerce and was nominated as business of the month. This opened up contacts that planted seeds for future business in the community. Sometimes you reap what you sow. Your efforts today might take months to pay off.

I wanted to branch out to nearby cities for more students and to get the word out about Simply Music. The closest town to me is nearly thirty miles away. My goal was one student and then hopefully it would take off from there. After a few months, my first student signed up. I suggested he try to recruit more students and I would commute one day a week to teach a group lesson. My student was thrilled with the idea and even offered for me to teach in his basement music room!

In September, I started a Back to School Piano Camp. I advertised it as a great way to try out Simply Music. I held it for four weeks and nineteen new students attended. Out of the nineteen, thirteen students continued with regular scheduled lessons. This was a profitable use of my time and good exposure for my studio.

Persistence really pays off. I presented a Free Introductory Session at our local Senior Center and an eighty-two-year-old gentleman approached me. I didn't know if he was interested in Simply Music, but he wanted me to help him 'get his two hands to work together'. Simply Music is a great way to do that. He wasn't too sure about the whole program and said that he was a very busy man. I followed up with him several times and he finally called me and wanted to check out the program. When I started playing some of the blues songs for him, his eyes just lit up! When he became my student, I realized never to give up. Sometimes, it takes effort, time, and energy, but it pays off.

Training and support amongst Simply Music teachers continues to inspire me and keep me motivated to build my studio. Conferences and the teacher's email/blog site have been beyond words of encouragement. It is so encouraging to hear all the teachers' ideas, stories, and struggles. Neil Moore, the founder of Simply Music, provides the vision through these media. I received so much helpful information that I can't say "thank you" enough to my fellow teachers. I am so grateful. Since starting Simply Music, I have never felt as if I am in a 'boat without a paddle'.

I am so glad that I am teaching Simply Music. It has been such an amazing experience these last five months. It has given me so much freedom to be who I am and to be able to be living out one of my dreams. The support has been so incredible. I might never want to do anything else! Starting the business has been so easy, too. Low costs, maximum support, immediate results. If you are not passionate about what you are doing right now, let me encourage you to look into this amazing program. Who wouldn't want to try?

§§§

Though I've only been teaching Simply Music for a few months, it has been enough time for me to see dramatic results in myself and my students, especially when compared to my teaching by traditional methods. The experience is a real win for everyone concerned. The musical results are undeniable for my students – we are all so pleased to have them playing such sophisticated music so quickly. Simply Music has been lucrative and frees me up to pursue other personal projects.

Mark S. Meritt, Simply Music Teacher
Red Hook, New York

CHAPTER 23

BUSINESS SAVVY

Why I Run a Large Studio

By Jy Gronner
Corte Madera, California

Jy Gronner studied piano in Oxford, England, and was trained in piano and conducting at the San Francisco Conservatory of Music. In addition, Jy earned a Bachelor of Fun Arts at the Ringling Bros. and Barnum & Bailey Circus Clown College in Florida. Jy's Simply Music studio has consistently averaged over one-hundred students since its inception. She loves to be a regular witness to the most ineffable joy expressed by students as they find new ways to express themselves emotionally, mentally, physically, and spiritually.

It's Not For Me

It all began with my sister. "You do it," I said to her, Sheri Reingold, now a successful Simply Music teacher. "I'll see what happens in *your* life." Sheri was telling me about Neil Moore and Simply Music, her great new discovery, and attempting to convince me to explore it for myself.

"Besides, it's bad timing," I continued, "so it couldn't be right for me." What I didn't say to her was that I didn't care to consider a profession that is basically valued at one of the lowest echelons of the societal totem pole. I was too proud to see beyond this bias. And my further conditioning as a conservatory-trained pianist dictated that a piano program that included 'keyboard' training, not to mention one that could be taught by Sheri, who had only had a few years of piano lessons as a child, couldn't be earth-shaking, to say the least! I was a *serious* musician. I was skeptical. And I didn't want to waste my time hearing about some new piano method.

It was also 'bad timing' because I was just starting a new business venture myself. I was forty and single, and it was time to start thinking seriously about earning more than just enough to live on. In managing various businesses throughout my life, I was adept at earning money for others. I had all but given up hope of finding a career wherein I would be not only intellectually stimulated and emotionally fulfilled, but also financially successful. It was time to plan further into my future than next month's rent. It was time to get serious.

Way Back When

I started piano lessons at age six, as did my four sisters. My teacher was 'traditional', like most piano teachers in the seventies. And like all students of traditional methods, I learned how to *read* music as a means of learning how to *play* music. Except for the proverbial annual student recital where performing from memory was mandatory, I did not learn to play the piano without written music in front of me.

As a child, I excelled in my piano studies. I attribute this partly to the prospect of practicing in exchange for an escape from nightly kitchen duty. My sisters all ended up gourmet cooks. I have a special talent for grilling open-faced cheese sandwiches. Joking aside, the "escape" allowed me regular breaks from the constant bustling energy and noise of my home life. I found solace in playing and was eager to learn new pieces.

So I continued through high school and college, studying piano and conducting at UCLA, in Oxford, England, and at the San Francisco Conservatory of Music. Following my formal studies, I gained diverse skills in various "careers": milking cows, guiding desert hikes and camping tours, managing a wholesale business, managing a retail business, fixing tractors, teaching Hebrew, teaching computer courses, training as a Ringling Brothers and Barnum & Bailey circus clown, owning and acting in a theatre troupe, directing and conducting choirs, teaching natural vision improvement, running corporate retreats, and more.

I always loved work. I viewed each job in my young adulthood more as a "mission" than a job. I believed in the organizations and companies that hired me and I took pride in my work. But until recently, I hadn't valued personal financial success enough to seek a livelihood that not only would be fulfilling to me, but would also allow me choices that are born out of financial abundance.

Simply Music – "Serious?"

I never, ever envisioned myself pursuing a full-time piano teaching career. Though I had been teaching piano for many years, I had always taught 'on the side', and felt I didn't 'fit the mold' of that profession namely, a housewife producing a second income for the family by teaching about ten students. I wasn't a housewife last time I checked – and I didn't have strong role models in my life of piano teachers who were not only professionally fulfilled, but who also earned the kind of living which I was now seriously seeking. I so enjoyed my stints as a teacher or choir director, or anything else involving music, but I did not see musicians around me earning a "serious" income even professional musicians. In my world, making *real* money as a musician was reserved for the famous.

Surprise!

So I sat on the sidelines and "watched" Sheri and her new Simply Music venture, while I proceeded to fully engage myself in my separate new business venture. But a few months after she opened her doors as a Simply Music teacher, I heard her students play and really couldn't believe my ears…her *beginning* students were playing popular, classical, blues, jazz, and accompaniment pieces with utter ease and musicality – and they were having a blast! I did a mental double-take – yes, it *had* only been a few short months!

And it was the fun *she* was having, not only with her teaching, but with her newly acquired (and incredible!) playing skills as well – not to mention her financial success – that enticed me to take a closer look at Simply Music. What I discovered was nothing short of extraordinary.

Simply Music is Creating a Revolution

I went to meet Neil Moore, the Australian creator of Simply Music. Neil is a man whose character, insight, wisdom, intelligence (genius, rather, I would say), accomplishments, and sheer talent are worthy of several volumes by themselves. His experience and background span many fields, and his expertise in so many areas – not to mention his extraordinary vision – account for the transformational force that is Simply Music.

Here is a human being who, against all odds, is rather single-handedly creating a revolution in how people express themselves, in how our culture defines musicality, in how we define the type of person who is capable of teaching music – that is, how any teacher can succeed in teaching virtually *any*body to play the piano.

Neil is accomplishing nothing short of changing the world! He is gradually proving that people can be transformed positively and profoundly when they unlock their ability to express themselves musically. Adult students and parents alike are attributing improvements in school, work, and other arenas to learning through this remarkable program.

Simply Music is gradually, but categorically, disproving the cultural illusions we have unconsciously inherited; that only some people are musical – only those who play an instrument or sing, and that you lost your opportunity if you didn't start learning at a young age, and that it takes a long time, and that you have to have a special talent, and, and…

My excitement soared as I learned how Simply Music is creating an entirely new paradigm – an altogether new standard in music-learning, music-playing, and music-teaching.

Deep down, I found myself aligned with Simply Music's premise that *everyone* is deeply, profoundly, and naturally musical. As Simply Music offers the possibility for the "masses" to experience their natural musicality, we are surely witnessing a revolution in the making.

The Stories Emerge

I heard more and more "miraculous" stories from my sister Sheri and met countless other teachers who had as many of their own...some with years of experience who had searched far and wide for a 'piano method that works'. Suddenly yes, suddenly, they were producing results far beyond what they had ever produced before, a quantum leap beyond what they ever considered possible. Parents were becoming more vocal as well, consistently conveying excitement with their kids' practicing habits; rather than forcing their children to practice, they were forcing them to stop playing and go to sleep! And some adult students were moved to tears at the happiness and deep fulfillment they were experiencing with their lessons. Unlocking this innate gift from inside our 'western psyches' was proving transformational for students and teachers alike, all over the world, all starting in the first lessons! Oh, where I would have been as a child after three years of Simply Music lessons!

Through learning more and more about brain function over the past century, we have changed the way we teach almost everything. Why not piano? How did we become so entrenched in a way of teaching that worked for so few, for so long a period of time? How could it be that until now no one – in three hundred years – had come up with a piano method that really works for everyone? How did we stray so far from our roots as human beings who were aware of our natural and easy relationship with playing music, as tribal peoples remain today?

In understanding the mechanics of how the teaching of piano has been structured for the last few centuries, coupled with exploration of the brain and how it best absorbs information in a learning environment, I realized that the struggle that has long been associated with playing the piano has nothing to do with 'playing the piano' and everything to do with how we have been *teaching* piano.

Possibilities

It suddenly dawned on me that I could become a Simply Music teacher – that I could play a role in actually transforming how people fundamentally see themselves! That I have a chance to impact their ability to enjoy their lives, increase their sense of confidence, and self-esteem; that, through making music, people could change their relationship to discipline, mental clarity, grief, sadness – the whole spectrum of human emotion. And that so many more people could benefit as I did: having music as a companion to bring joy and relaxation, and to ease life's struggles...indeed, be a cause of exhilaration and help change their entire outlook on life! I knew this was possible and I felt a deep sense of purpose in making the decision to become a Simply Music teacher.

I saw how impactful Simply Music was to my sister, her students, and the teachers I met. I felt strongly compelled to create an environment whereby I could in turn positively impact the lives of a large number of people. I wanted to use my "working" time to do something truly meaningful. I wanted to create a center full of joy, and playing, and the sound of music. I wanted to create a workplace for myself that was alive and where I felt alive every day.

Furthermore, I finally found an opportunity not only to be intellectually, emotionally, and creatively fulfilled, but also to earn the kind of money and live the kind of life I sought and dreamed about. I wanted to have more free time and more financial freedom. Not to mention that I could simply choose to 'opt out' of the rat race most of our society seemed to be in!

Indeed, I could feel alive with Simply Music into a ripe old age! This was a dynamic and growing company, but what was so exciting was that a Simply Music career wasn't one I would easily 'grow out of'. I could teach until I could no longer speak! How many careers have the kind of longevity whereby one could continue to profit, both personally and financially, into old age? I could always have Simply Music as a part- or full-time career, happily and successfully and comfortably teaching into my eighties, as my teacher at UCLA had! I found myself truly inspired – I wanted to share this with as many people as possible! Realizing that so many of my dreams could be fulfilled through becoming a Simply Music teacher seemed almost too miraculous to be true.

Taking the Plunge

The following year (now unabashedly impressed and intrigued by Sheri's success), I left my new business behind and moved to beautiful Marin County, in California. I started talking to everyone I met about this remarkable program I was learning about more and more each day. As excitement goes, mine was infectious! I didn't care if people said "yes" or "no". I just had to share my discovery. I wanted a Simply Music studio and I wanted it fast.

My plan was to start "seeing" myself as already successful in my business. In the past, I had experienced that if I visualized my success, using all my senses, that I could create it. So I set out doing just that. From the beginning, it was miracle after miracle. I was encouraged by the message I seemed to be getting: I was on the right path!

First I needed to decide in which community to live, and then find a nice commercial space – complete with enough parking for the Free Introductory Sessions (which I decided would be larger than the lessons!), not too far from the freeway, but not too close, the center of the county and certainly cheap enough to pay back the money I borrowed for rent with my first month's teaching income. It would also have to be the first place I looked at, since my time was limited! I filled in the rest of the blanks in the sensory imagery exercise: how it would look, how it would sound, how it would smell, how it would feel, etc.

The first miracle occurred in finding the studio space. Not only did I find, on the very first attempt, *the* perfect location – quiet, but not so quiet that other businesses would be bothered by children's laughter and the sound of the piano, the perfect distance (about a half mile) from the freeway, and a *huge* park as a backyard (ideal for the much-favored Frisbee breaks) – but I also got perhaps the deal of the millennium! A whole story in itself. I knew that I was on the right track.

Finding the First Students

I was more and more excited with each passing day. I assembled my studio furniture, rented a piano, and set up my office. I found to my delight that Simply Music not only provides a fully structured program and a long-term curriculum, but also all the business and teaching materials that I might need, including sample ads, based on years of thoughtful research. I downloaded all the forms I would need for teaching and running the business, and crunched numbers to figure out how many students I would need to cover my first month's rent in the new space, including all the expenses I had incurred to date. I wanted to make a profit in my very first month, so I tripled the number of students I would need. This was fun!

I needed forty-four students and I set a deadline for myself. I had two months to meet enough people to enroll at least forty-four of them. I did Free Introductory Sessions two or three times a week and talked on the phone. It felt good. It all happened so fast!

Soon I opened my doors with exactly forty-four students! Over the next few years I employed other Simply Music teachers and grew to over two-hundred-fifty students. I currently maintain my own studio of about one-hundred-twenty-five students and I help other Simply Music teachers with their new businesses. I'm still pinching myself as to the ease in which I achieved a dream: I enjoy a part-time teaching schedule with a full-time income!

From the very beginning, I decided to view my business as the *life* I wanted to lead, not merely a way of earning a living. I knew that if I enjoyed the process, I would have success. And I wanted to enjoy my life! So I put two and two together, and *voila!* I put my efforts into creating as much fun and ease as possible into my new endeavor.

Setting up business was also exciting because of the confidence that I would succeed – Simply Music's training materials basically dictate success!

I knew that when someone initially said "no" to my invitation to share Simply Music, there was usually a lesson in it for me. I honed my skills and learned that when I was able to connect with my desire to simply share an amazing discovery, rather than having to 'get people's business', I found that almost everyone I approached had a dream of wanting to play the piano somewhere deep inside.

Many adults first said "no" because they had a picture in their minds of it being very difficult to play the piano. But when I "dug" just a bit, I found that many were pulling something out from inside of themselves that they had not expected to reveal – even to themselves! It was sad, but made a lot of sense that so many people had suppressed their dream to play the piano. I started hearing a pattern in the stories: traditional lessons as children or adults, almost no success whatsoever, and definitely not fun.

So, instead of feeling like I was selling something, I found that I was constantly finding opportunities to simply share a "secret" that could, in many senses, free people and begin to allow them to heal parts of themselves that were not completely healthy. I began to feel that I almost couldn't keep it from people – that if I didn't share what I knew, I was being selfish!

I came up with a short phrase in case I only had a few seconds to grab someone's attention. I came up with a sentence or two if I had a bit more time, and a longer conversation if there was even more initial interest. I memorized the Free Introductory Session that Neil included in the training materials. This gave me access to so many "conversations", and inspired me even more to share what I was learning.

A Large Studio: Turn-Key Business, Turn-Key Results

I wanted to succeed (really, I needed to succeed). I knew that simply 'following the program' would create optimal results, in all ways: not only for my students, but for my own growth as a person and business owner. I learned that one of the components of Simply Music's success is the shared lesson environment as a more effective learning framework. I learned that students in Simply Music studios around the world in a shared lesson environment were producing superior results compared to those in private lessons – consistently – over and over again.

As a 'traditionalist', before learning about Simply Music, I hadn't imagined that one could successfully learn piano in a group setting. I, like those around me, grew up with the cultural notion of private, traditional piano lessons as the only way to learn how to play. But I wanted what would be best for my students and I knew that would also, in turn, help create my business success. I realized that there were two wonderful by-products of teaching in groups. From the students' perspective, my rates could be competitive – I could even set them lower than the going rate in the county! And from the teacher's perspective, I could earn more money in less "teaching" time. On top of that, my students would produce better results!

Fine, but why was the shared lesson more effective? If I was to convince parents and potential adult students of this, I had better understand it myself! The shared lesson environment in Simply Music is such a dynamic learning environment because it involves not only participation, but also observation. Humans learn most naturally by observing – that is how we learn to walk, talk, eat, and become adults. In Simply Music, we merge *receptive* learning with *generative* learning – hands-on learning – for a balanced, whole-brain, more profound learning experience.

The shared lesson is so compelling – it's motivating. Students are actively engaged in various aspects of the program at any given time. The activity changes every few minutes. There is a lot of exchange – back and forth, input, output, questions, answers, other answers...a lot of sound and a lot of music! Without actively or knowingly teaching, all students become teachers in the lesson, and having so much exchange contributes to more learning – subliminal, and otherwise.

Simply Music students are playing together, in ensemble, from the very first lessons. This alone is such a powerful learning tool! My students come to realize that what they experience in Simply Music lessons – playing with others – is an activity that is so compelling that they find they are continually drawn to various ensemble playing opportunities outside of their lessons. How exciting as teachers to see students making great music with others, being able to adapt so well to diverse musical situations. As Simply Music teachers, we can unlock such a profound gift in our students – an opportunity for a lifetime of fulfillment – socially, emotionally, intellectually, and spiritually …how wonderful to have piano playing as a lifelong companion!

After learning about the incredible results of the shared lesson environment, I realized I couldn't ignore the opportunity to share the joyous – and in countless cases, exhilarating – feelings that come with this experience. Why not build a studio?

How wonderful that the most efficient way to earn more money in Simply Music is to teach in a way that produces better results for students anyway! How could I pass up an opportunity to earn more money in fewer hours of teaching? Simply Music provides the "blueprint" for my success? The shared lesson was the way to go! I found that I would reach new heights as a teacher, as a business owner, and as a person. And it all happened just as I had envisioned!

The Business Grows as the Business Grows

Word-of-mouth marketing is the most powerful form of marketing. Marketing a Simply Music studio becomes more effortless the more students there are to talk about it. I found this alone contributes greatly to the growth of my studio.

When students begin lessons, friends hear about it, neighbors hear them playing, siblings see their older sisters and brothers enjoying it so much. After my first "batch" of students, the phone started ringing more. So, the larger my studio became, the faster my business was able to grow.

I was even more excited when I discovered that there are so many avenues of expression through having a Simply Music business. If I ever got bored with one aspect of the business, there would be ample opportunity to switch lanes and create a new way of expressing myself professionally.

I hired other teachers, so I had even more freedom to grow the business and find more personal growth opportunities, not only musically though there were endless possibilities there, but also with helping other teachers.

The Power of Enjoyment

Today, I am proud to be actively participating in the Simply Music "revolution". I am routinely and enthusiastically disproving the cultural illusions we have inherited around piano lessons. In the past five years, I've successfully taught students of all ages (five to ninety-one), students of all backgrounds (musical and otherwise), students who swore that they were not "musical", and students who had no "special talent". I have witnessed immediate results across the board with all who have followed the program.

And the lessons are so fun! Adults have the highlight of their week with their lesson-mates. Many become friends outside the lesson, and meet to play and practice together. Kids have piano play-dates! They love learning with their friends and making new ones, and are smiling and laughing at their lessons. I get to watch parents who are in awe of their children on a daily basis and adult students excited beyond their expectations. I have seen students motivate themselves to learn on account of simply feeling *good*.

Indeed, one of Simply Music's declared goals is that we produce students who have a highly positive experience of *themselves* throughout the learning process...it's easy to feel good about yourself as a student (not to mention as a teacher) because it is an easy learning process; it's easy to progress from one step to the next. It's easy to develop an "emotional habit of success", as Neil Moore phrases it. That habit creates more confidence, which in turn increases the ability to take in more information, thereby ensuring more success – and it goes on and on.

I discovered another great by-product of teaching a large number of people – they positively affect an even larger number of people. A ripple effect is created by students influencing others through their playing. And students continue to grow at home through teaching others (a very powerful learning strategy); siblings learn, grandparents learn, and the "teacher" learns. It not only gives them a feeling of "I can change the world", but they realize that they *are* changing the world! Taking part in this kind of revolution empowers people.

Each day I go home knowing that I made an impact on my students – their intellect, emotional growth, social development – indeed, I can really *see* it happening each day. When I sought for a career that would be fulfilling, fun, profitable, freeing, and impactful for many, I truly got what I asked for.

§§§

Marketing Simply Music is quite easy. You have an advantage in the 'piano-lessons-marketplace' because of the unique selling points that Simply Music offers. Specifically, that students play classical, blues, jazz, pop, arrangements, and accompaniments from their very first lessons. Once people understand what you are offering them and believe it, they will be lining up to be your students!

Robin Keehn, Simply Music Teacher, Owner of Aspire Studio with over ninety Simply Music students
Sequim, Washington

CHAPTER 24

A LEADER WITH
A VISION

simply music

An Interview with Neil Moore

By Bernadette E. Ashby

Walking into the Simply Music headquarters is an experience in itself. From the outside, it is your typical office building: painted in neutral colors, manicured landscape, parking lot peppered with cars. But there is a twist when crossing the Simply Music threshold. You get the sense that something is uniquely different, daringly focused. There is something noticeable in the air. Clarity of thinking. Simplicity. Freedom.

Interestingly enough, the first smile that greets you belongs to a bronze metal wall hanging. It is the Simply Music logo. This iconic logo radiates warmth. The foyer is simple: a couch, coffee table, and an uncluttered welcome desk. Not just uncluttered – spotless! On the desk is a lone red rose outfitted in a simple vase. And a white Mac laptop. The room is immaculately pristine and ordered. Jazz music is playing in the background. From room to room, it is no different: clean, clear of any distractions, and simple. Why is the environment of the world's largest playing-based music institution so unencumbered? The answer is found in the person of Neil Moore, the Founder and Executive Director of Simply Music.

For Neil Moore, it is critical that the mind, soul, and heart of a person be free of any unwarranted distractions so that creativity and expression can freely flow. This kind of mindset sets Neil Moore apart from others. His vision drives Simply Music to be on the cutting edge of music education.

Neil Moore is the visionary who has set Simply Music in motion. That vision is a growing movement that is changing the face of music education. In this interview with Neil Moore, you will gain a sense of his desire to spread the message about Simply Music and his vision, "a world where everyone plays".

B: Neil, what does it take to have vision?

N: I think that it is really important to draw a distinction between the words "vision" and "imagination". Obviously, it's tremendously important to have imagination. I think a vivid imagination is a wonderful thing. But commonly, when people think in terms of vision, they think about it in terms of something mystical. I don't see it like that. There's an enormous difference between having a vivid imagination and being a visionary, yet one is merely the manifestation of the other. A visionary is someone that has a vivid imagination, but they act upon their imagination in a different manner. I say there are five things that are at the core of action for every visionary. A visionary has a clear picture of the vision itself, a vision that can be imagined and foreseen. They have the ability to clearly articulate the vision to others. They have the ability to enroll people to a degree whereby, of their own volition, they consistently enroll others in the vision. They have the ability to identify and generate whatever resources are needed to fulfill the vision. Most importantly, they have an unstoppable commitment to fulfill the vision regardless of the circumstances, the conditions, or the story. So in terms of Simply Music, this is a possibility that needs to be both spoken and "actioned" into existence. In terms of the bigger picture, I see us assembling whatever resources are needed in order to disseminate this program on a global basis, taking it into third-world nations, doing far-reaching philanthropic work, introducing the method as an education platform throughout other countries, setting up music schools and institutes of higher learning, taking it into inner-city schools. These are all just a few possibilities. Alternately, this is a vision of the world where everyone plays.

B: How did Simply Music come into being?
N: There are many layers to answering this fully, but in the simplest of terms, Simply Music came about as a result of two things. One, my own background, my own history of playing. The other, an experience that I had teaching a boy called Wade.

B: Who is Wade?
N: Wade was an eight-year-old boy who was blind and I was given the opportunity to teach him how to play. I was the head of another music teaching institution that taught a reading-based approach. I received a call one day from a government agency. I can't remember what agency it was, but the woman I spoke to asked if I would be willing to take on this young boy who was

without sight. I think that the agency was somehow involved with funding a new type of surgery that they thought could restore his sight. I also think that the agency was going to fund the piano lessons for the family. I don't know how they heard about me, but when they called and asked if I could teach the boy how to play, obviously I said, "Yes." Given that Wade was without sight, reading music would be out of the question. But looking back on my own experience of learning music I thought to myself, "I never learned to read when I was young; why don't I see if I can teach him to play in a similar manner to how I learned myself as a boy."

B: How did you learn as a child?
N: I was the youngest of five children, four boys and one girl. My sister studied elocution as a child, however, the four boys all started piano lessons as we each turned seven. Our teacher was a very accomplished musician with a great understanding of both classical and contemporary music. He taught an entirely reading-based approach. By the time I was born, there were already piano lessons going on in the home, and by the time I was three or four years old, I would hear music and picture it in my mind in terms of shapes and patterns. When I started piano lessons at seven, and my teacher would play the songs I was to be learning, I would also see what he was playing on the keyboard in terms of shapes and patterns. Seeing music this way was entirely natural for me and it immediately gave me access to being able to play the songs. The funny thing was that, in my mind, I thought that I was doing something wrong with seeing music this way. I thought that if my teacher found out that I wasn't reading, I'd get into trouble. At my lessons on Saturday mornings, I would sit at the piano and play, as I would stare blankly at the music in front of me, pretending to read. My teacher never said anything. My ability to play the songs

was entirely based on my aural relationship and my natural ability to see music in terms of shapes and patterns. The printed music on the page meant absolutely nothing to me whatsoever.

B: How did your parents handle your lack of reading ability?

N: What I didn't know was that my teacher had spoken to my mother and told her that I wasn't reading, that I was just pretending to read. Thankfully, my mother had said to my teacher, "but listen to how well he is playing, just let him do his own thing." So for the next eight years, I had lessons every week and I practiced every day. I never thought of it as a burden, it was simply a family requirement. Throughout this time, I still never learned to read. All of my older brothers were reading music, but I couldn't read a note. It was never discussed between myself and my teacher, or my parents, and, even though I was playing well, I still believed I was doing something wrong and that I was hiding something. Actually, I was quite ashamed of myself. In fact, throughout my teens and even as an adult, I didn't tell people that I played. I kept it as a very private thing because I thought that people would pull out some sheet music and ask me to play. I was terrified that I would be 'found out'. I thought that my approach to learning music, seeing things so naturally and organically in terms of shapes and patterns on a keyboard, was sort of "fraudulent". Truthfully, I didn't learn how to read music until my early thirties. I also didn't learn about classical theory until I began formal music studies around the same time.

B: So how did you apply your perspective into this new approach?

N: Well, when I began teaching Wade, I asked myself for the first time, "How did I actually learn to play when I was young?"

Even though I saw things in term of shapes and patterns, I never consciously thought about it, it was just who I was. So I started to look more closely to my own relationship to learning and began to reconstruct it for myself, consciously bringing language to what it was that I was doing. Then, I would take pieces of music, break them down into shapes and patterns and present them to Wade. Within about three months, he was playing a repertoire of about twelve to fifteen songs. One day, I asked Wade's father if he was happy with how the piano lessons were going. Wade's dad told me that they were thrilled and that Wade had begun to teach his four-year-old sister how to play and she, too, was blind. That really blew me away! It was a major turning point in my life. I didn't really know what had happened. I just knew that something had happened and that things were never going to be the same. At the time, I really had no idea what I had in my hands.

B: What happened next?
N: I thought to myself, "I wonder what would happen if I taught all children this way?" Even then, I was still only thinking of this in terms of it being almost like 'music orientation' or 'music pre-school' – a place to start before students progressed to *real* music, which at that time, I still considered to be learning how to read. Now looking back at it, my thinking was ridiculous! Reading music had had no bearing whatsoever on the way that I had learned to play. Yet for some reason, in my mind, it was real for me that reading music was the way it was "supposed" to be done. So it was really eye opening for me when I began sharing my approach with other young children. It wasn't just the quantity of music that these children were playing; it was also how quickly they were learning. Another thing that struck me was their natural relationship to playing. They were so free in their relationship to their music.

B: What did you do with these results?

N: I started sharing the concepts with other teachers to see if they could replicate the results. They started to say the same thing; they were seeing the same results. So I took about one-hundred-and-twenty-five students and over an extended period of time, I began exploring how far I could take this approach. Would it apply to all sorts of musical styles: contemporary, gospel, blues, jazz, classical, etc? How far could I take it before I really had to introduce music reading? I wanted to see how far I could really go without relying on anything other than a playing-based approach to music. Over time, I road tested, monitored the results, created, and codified a curriculum.

B: How did you codify the results?

N: That in itself was rather a remarkable experience. I'd take a piece of music and I'd come up with a playing-based strategy. Let's say it was now Monday morning. Over the next day or two, I would teach it in thirty different classes to thirty different students. I learned a lot from that because these students came from different backgrounds, were at different levels in their musicianship and were different ages. I would observe how they were learning, I'd make changes, and then I'd teach the new approach to a different group of thirty students in different classes. The results would improve and I would continue to observe. I would make some more changes to the approach and then I'd teach to a completely different group of thirty students. I would see further improvement in how quickly and easily students were learning. Usually by this time, I would have figured out what seemed to be an ideal strategy or approach to teaching the song I was focusing on. There might just be a few adjustments to make. So, I'd tweak the approach a little bit more and then teach the 'final product', so to speak, to another group of thirty students. Finally, by this time, I'd arrived at an approach to teaching this song that I was confident would pretty much work for any and everybody. The beauty in doing it this way was that all of this would take place in just one week. Every ten weeks, I would have taught another one-thousand-two-hundred-and-fifty lessons. For me, teaching nearly six-and-a-half-thousand lessons per year, I learned so much from the entire experience working with beginning and more advanced students, children, teens, adults, and seniors. Yet, even though that entire experience became the foundation for codifying the curriculum, ultimately, all of what I was doing was based on my lifelong relationship to music – seeing shapes and patterns in everything.

B: You've mentioned the words 'playing-based' many times? What does that mean?

N: In a traditional environment, the prevailing approach is that students start by firstly learning how to read music. I call that a 'reading-based' approach. It is profoundly different than Simply Music. In our program, everything that we do is based on the foundation of playing. Long before a student begins reading, they have built a repertoire of thirty, forty, fifty songs or more. All of this was learned through a direct connection to the instrument. We teach students to play by actually having them play. It's learning by doing. And it is the same across the entire curriculum. Everything we teach, whether it be scale, key signature, chords, the circle of fifths, transposition, arranging, lead sheets, as well as reading and writing music, etc., is based on a foundation of playing.

B: When did you start Simply Music as a business?
N: In January of 1998, Simply Music officially came into being. I launched it as the first generation of the program called TP1, 'Teacher Program 1'.

B: How did it expand?
N: I saw this process as something not only I could do, but others could replicate. As people were learning from the program, they were inheriting the ability to teach other family members. I just knew that there were legions of people out there that wanted and needed something like this. I recognized that this was the heart of an organization; a viable opportunity to contribute to people and, at the same time, generate resources that could fuel the building of an infrastructure.

B: What are the critical components of the method?
N: This is simplified, but the critical components of the method are the body of tools, the approaches, the domains of learning, and the management of the relationship to learning.

B: Tell me about the tools?
N: Tools are a critical component in Simply Music. There's a whole variety of tools, but essentially they center around seeing music in terms of shapes, patterns, sentences, fragments, maps, etc., as well as seeing how all of these are organized and ordered.

B: Tell me more about approaches.
N: Once again, this is a simplified overview, but it could be said that human beings learn in two fundamental realms: one is the realm of 'receptive learning' and the other is 'generative learning'. Receptive is where we are receiving instruction from an external

source, learning by receiving instructions. Generative learning is where we can generate the learning for ourselves, where we actually create for ourselves the learning that needs to take place.

In Simply Music, we're always mindful of the learning realm that is being utilized. With that in mind, we break down the steps of learning into further concepts we arrive at what I call 'Approaches'. Approaches are things that help us learn. One example, of many, might be the concept of 'controlling the events'. This is the physical requirement to slow down a student's movement in their hands and fingers to such a speed that the brain can process and create a very clear neural pathway between what it wants to do and what it physically needs to do in order to execute something. Another 'approach' might involve distilling things into 'single thought processes'. This is actually a critical approach in the Simply Music method. Other approaches include 'creating micro-events', employing 'multi-sensory layering' etc. There are many approaches within the method and they continue to unfold as students move more deeply into the curriculum.

B: What about domains?

N: Domains are a continuation within the realms I mentioned earlier. Essentially, they're further conceptualized approaches to learning. An example of this would be what we call 'observatory learning' – this is where one observes what needs to be learned, and, through nothing other than the observation, program their neurology and physiology. I think that many people make an error of judgment in believing that the observation of something is quite passive. I am saying that it goes much deeper than that. The wiring/connectivity between what is happening neurologically and physiologically can actually take place merely as a function of observing something as it

229

happens. This is a powerful process! Another example of a domain would be 'participatory learning'. This is where one is actually executing what needs to be learned. In any learning environment, there are different types of learning that are occurring.

B: Can you give me an example of participatory/ observatory learning?

N: Sure. This is something that we see in Shared Lessons where a group of students are learning at one time. Let's say that I have ten students in a lesson. I sit down at the piano and show them what to do. Let's say that it is a rather complex physical thing that I am asking them to do. The first student then has an opportunity to play. The actual act of playing is, by definition, Participatory Learning. In the background, however, I can see on my student's faces that they, too, are going through the mental wiring – the necessary neurology, the pathways in the brain, that need to connect in order to create the appropriate physiology. Quite wonderfully, by the time the second student plays, there is less that needs to be learned. By the time I get to the third, fourth, fifth student, even though they haven't played yet, by merely watching others play you can clearly see that an enormous amount of physical learning has already taken place, solely as a function of the observation. I think that this is really remarkable! Incidentally, I do need to mention that I use this terminology and language, intuitively and anecdotally. As an organization, we haven't yet built a body of empirical data to fully explain this, but I stand by my assertions.

B: Okay, you've covered tools, approaches, and domains. What about the relationship to learning?

N: Firstly, when I say 'relationship', I'm not talking about how you get along with people. What I am talking about is the critical need to understand that if you are to have music as a life-long companion, then you'll need to enter into a long-term relationship with music. If you're going to enter into a life-long relationship, then it makes sense for us to examine the nature, and characteristics of long-term relationships. I say that all long-term relationships have certain components and idiosyncrasies that exist in *every* long-term relationship. Not only do these need to be clearly understood, but a unique approach as to how these are managed needs to be present throughout the entire learning experience. The Simply Music experience includes learning how to manage the long-term experience. We have distinguished a means of relating to the commonality between people with regard to their relationship to the actual process and experience of learning.

B: Anything else you want to say about that?
N: There's a lot more to say about that, but I'm not sure that it's appropriate right now. Winston Churchill responded to a similar question once. He said something like, "If you want me to talk for an hour, I'm ready to go now, but if you want me to talk for two minutes, I need two weeks to prepare."

B: Okay, what are some of the differences between Simply Music and other methods?
N: Well, there are many, many differences. Here's a few. Firstly, Simply Music is what we call a 'playing-based methodology'. This is a unique distinction and, to my knowledge, we are the only music education institution that operates in this arena. With regard to the method, the first most obvious difference is that we delay the music reading process. Everything we do is based on a foundation of playing. We firstly teach students how to play by applying the various tools, approaches, use of domains, and the

management of the relationship to learning. Secondly, we are unique in that we fall outside of the traditional demographics where 95% of students who learn music are between five and twelve years of age. For us, more than a third of our students are between thirty-five and ninety five years of age! We go right across the board. Thirdly, it appears that we are able to make inroads into areas that traditional programs have had less success with. For example, we can consistently produce outstanding results with those that are dealing with ADD, ADHD, autism, turrets, blindness, and deafness. We are not yet exactly sure why this program is able to make such inroads in these areas, but the results that we see are quite remarkable. Fourthly, we redefine who is capable of playing music and who is capable of teaching music. At the most practical level, probably the main difference with Simply Music and other methods is the enormity of the repertoire, the quantity of music, and the quality of music students learn, how quickly they learn, and how easily they learn.

B: That's a lot of differences! What should a parent be thinking about with their child's music education? What questions should they ask?

N: The first question I think that a parent should ask of themselves is, "Why do you want your child to have music in their life?" and, "What is it that you want for them?" As a parent, are you coming into this with a commitment for your child to elevate to adult, concert-level performance? If so, "Is that really what you want?" or, "Do you want to give your child the best opportunity possible where they can maximize the likelihood of acquiring and retaining music as a companion for the rest of their lives?" If the goal is for self-expression through music to be a lifelong companion, then we need to revolutionize the prevailing approach to music education.

B: What makes Simply Music a better way to go?

N: Simply Music allows everybody to immediately experience their natural musicianship. And there is no question that it's worth the investment of learning how to navigate your way through the peaks, plateaus, and valleys of the long-term relationship in order to retain self expression through music throughout one's life. I think we do this better than anybody and that our approach to how we do this is unique. It also seems that the Simply Music experience is vastly different than the average experience of most students who learn with traditional methods. It seems that so many students have to go through years of grueling discipline and focused effort and, even then, often don't experience a natural relationship with the expression of their own musicality. In so many ways there are profound differences with Simply Music. In essence, if you want an immediate experience of your musicianship, if you want to build a phenomenal foundation of moving on to more advanced levels, if you want to have an fantastic experience of yourself, a really positive and affirming experience of yourself, and achieve all of that in the midst of playing all sorts of musical genres, then this is fundamentally what Simply Music provides. Simply Music pretty much achieves this routinely with each and every student.

B: What is the experience like for a child in the program?

N: Firstly, it is critical to understand how important it is for a child to play. In the world of a child, playing is the child's equivalent of an adult's work or career or vocation. Playing and playfulness for a child develops their neurology, physiology, psychology, and sociology. Playing develops their creativity, their self-expression, their individuality, and their spirituality. It impacts everything, both the humanness

233

and the being in their lives. With Simply Music, children experience playing from their very first lessons: they develop a strong, natural connection with their innate musicality – this alone is profound. In addition to this, the nature of our learning environment and the way in which we engage the parent allows the child to explore and develop a relationship with discipline, responsibility, life requirements, personal and parental values, commitment, accomplishment – all of those things that play out in any and every endeavor that they will participate in for the rest of their lives.

B: What is important for you to communicate to a child?

N: When I teach, my fundamental commitment is that every child experiences how important I consider them to be. I'm committed that every child experiences how highly I regard them and that I respect them. For me, this is a critical context to create, one that fundamentally impacts who they are, who they consider themselves to be, and, of course, their entire learning experience.

B: How is a child's experience with Simply Music different than with traditional music lessons?

N: This is not necessarily an easy question to answer. However, if I were to look at the average student, having an average experience with the average teacher, using the average traditional approach, then there does appear to be a consistent type of experience. Commonly, children who learn traditionally are evaluated to determine whether they have any 'musical talent' or not. In fact, for a great many children, this alone becomes a defining moment that they carry with them for the rest of their lives. We teach a great many students who have been bruised, often scarred, by this experience. Simply Music, in contrast, is based on the premise that absolutely everybody, without exception, is profoundly musical. With that as a context, all we need to do is 'dis-cover', uncover the natural musicality that is rampant in everybody.

Also, in the traditional environment, there is clearly a much higher degree of technical analysis. Most commonly, the focus is going to include, from the outset, learning how to read music, learning the theory of music, and usually a high emphasis on precise execution, perfection, and getting the physicality absolutely correct, i.e., technique. Most adults who talk about their experience learning music as a child say that it ranged from being anything between an ordinary experience to something that they absolutely hated. I'm sure that is not the case for all children that learn traditionally, but if we speak the truth, there are far too many people for whom this was, and still is, the case. Unfortunately, that "average" experience that I mentioned earlier is usually described by people as being arduous, difficult, not exciting, not invigorating, not playful. And clearly, from what I've seen over decades, it is just not the norm in the traditional experience for students to routinely and immediately experience their musicianship and retain a natural connection to it.

B: How do new parents like Simply Music?
N: Well, for parents and students that have no prior music background, they have nothing to compare Simply Music to. As you can imagine, they think that their experience in Simply Music is the normal experience for *anybody* learning music. The parent or student, who has never had lessons before, thinks it is the norm to be learning a new song every week, or two. Obviously, they love the fact their child is playing. And, of

course, having nothing else to compare it to, they come to expect these results and assume that this is what happens for everybody when they take piano lessons. Truthfully, I love the normalcy that inexperienced, uneducated musicians bring to this.

B: What is the role of the parent in a child's learning?
N: Firstly, in the traditional world, it's quite common for the parent to drop the child off at lessons. Commonly, the parent is not engaged in the actual learning process and this sets up a condition where parents come to believe that they are not responsible in the process. It also sets up the illusion that the music teacher is entirely responsible, for not only presenting the content, but also inspiring the child to practice over the course of the week. I say there is a critical design flaw in this structure.

In Simply Music, the role of the parent is critical. We create a three-way relationship between the teacher, the student, and the parent. There are particular and subtle skills that are needed in order to successfully manage this three-way relationship and it is a critical component of the Simply Music program. Managing this relationship is a permanent condition, fundamental to the entire Simply Music experience.

B: What happens if a parent is not involved in their child's learning?
N: Well, and this applies to any endeavor, the natural condition for a child is to base what they do on what they want to do or what they feel like doing. If there is no framework that teaches the child to see things differently, it will become habitual for them to base their commitment to anything on what they want to do or what they feel like doing. The problem with any commitment being based on feelings

236

and wants is that the moment that one doesn't want to do something, or doesn't feel like doing something, then the commitment goes out the window as well. In the absence of any structure designed to teach a child about the nature of commitment, i.e., if a parent is not overseeing the child's learning as well as their practice, then the child will only practice if they feel like it or want it. This is a setup for music learning to be a short-term experience. And it is a setup that is most common in a traditional environment.

You can imagine what the scenario looks like: parent drops off the child at lessons and is not engaged in the lesson, the child goes home and doesn't want to practice, often the parent is left feeling they have to force their child to practice and they soon tire of that. The child then is doing very limited practice. They go back to the teacher next week and the teacher sees little or no progress. After a while, the teacher gets tired of the situation and tells the parent that the child doesn't have any musical talent, ability, or commitment. And sooner or later, usually sooner, the child quits and more often than not, carries with them the experience of having failed at music. Often that failed experience comes with a decision about themselves where they believe they are not musical. It is staggering how common a version of this type of experience occurs. It's really strange. It so misses the mark of what is really going on. If parents really understood the enormity of the opportunity of having musical self-expression as a life long companion, I really think they would be far more willing to play an active role in the music learning experience of the child.

B: What does a parent need to understand?
N: If a parent truly wants their child to have music as a lifelong companion, then the first thing they need to understand is that

the child will have to learn how to navigate their way through a long-term relationship. And, that being the case, the parents need to understand what it looks like for a child who is learning how to have a long-term relationship. A parent can never expect a child to know how to navigate through a long-term relationship when the child hasn't had one. We could say that every long-term relationship, regardless of the field of endeavor, has six components at its core. These components are concepts. Three of them relate to "quality", and three of them relate to "quantity", or duration. The three "quality" components I just label as "peaks", "plateaus", and "valleys". In other words: good times, average times, and not so good times. The three components of "quantity", or duration, I just label as "brief", "sustained", or "prolonged". In other words: a short period of time, a sustained period of time, or a very much longer period of time. If we are to look at every long-term relationship, regardless of what it is, in some way, shape or form, it will consist of a series of peaks, plateaus, and valleys, over brief, sustained, or prolonged periods of time. We could crudely say that it would look something like a stock market graph over decades.

Typically, when things aren't going well, particularly if it is for a sustained or prolonged period of time, people begin to think that something is "wrong". Whereas, in fact, every long-term relationship has the condition of peaks, plateaus, and valleys that everybody needs to learn how to navigate their way through in order for that experience to *become* a long-term relationship. Mastery in navigating long-term relationships is all about learning how to remain committed, in action, to one's commitment, during those times when one doesn't feel like it and doesn't want to. The parent has a unique opportunity to play an extraordinary role in teaching their child how to navigate any and every long-term relationship their child enters into for the remainder of their lives. I often think of it like a racetrack: if the student is the car, the method and the teacher are the track itself. The parent is the fence on either side of the track. I'm happy for the child to head down the track and even bounce against the sides of the fence. But the fence, nonetheless, holds them on track. After a while, the child gets the hang of driving down the track, steering down the track, and they begin to develop the ability to self-generate their commitment. Parents have a unique opportunity in what they can provide in this area.

B: So it becomes an issue of training the parents?
N: Absolutely, even though it might be the child who is attending lessons, it is the parent that is always the student. This is always about educating the parent.

LONG-TERM RELATIONSHIP GRAPH

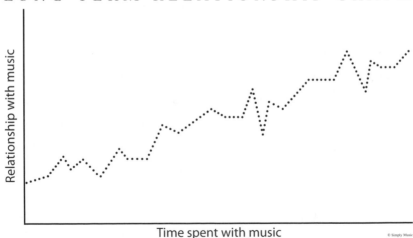

© Simply Music

B: How do adult students like Simply Music?

N: I've always loved teaching adults; particularly those that have had lessons before, and especially those that had lessons before and believed they failed. That person is typically blown away by Simply Music. It's really common for them to say things like, "This is life altering," or "This has blown my socks off," or "Unbelievable," when describing the Simply Music method. It is also very common for adults to become very emotional, particularly in the early stages. Often, they have had years of grueling lessons, where they were left feeling they had no talent or ability. Commonly, they were told this by a prior music teacher and then believed it to be true. Most often, what happens is that person continues to long to express themselves musically, but they deny themselves of that because they truly believe there is no point. They truly believe they have no musical ability. What's more, they have evidence of that because, after all, they did "try" in the past and they "failed". However, what can't be denied is that the longing to be musically self-expressed is innate, universal, and lifelong. Unfortunately, we live in a world where its common for entire cultures to have very little or no access to individual musical self expression.

I suggest that the absence of musical self-expression creates cultural conditions of very deep-seated, repressed frustration, which we have become so used to that it's just like white noise in the background that we no longer pay attention to. For the adult that comes to Simply Music, who then immediately starts playing great sounding pieces, they're commonly moved to tears. Sometimes those tears are an expression of release and relief. Other times the tears are a function of upset – the realization that they went through years or decades of needless pain. You can imagine how freeing it is for an adult to see that they need not have gone through that pain, that their failings had nothing to do with them as a person, that they weren't incomplete, and that they are, in fact, deeply and profoundly musical. You can imagine it is a pretty exciting experience for the average person who has had an average traditional experience, to then experience Simply Music. For them, it's commonly both a revelation and a transformation.

B: What types of students do best with Simply Music?
N: Students that are coachable. Coachablity is everything. In some respects, all sorts of things can be going on in a person's life, but if they are coachable, they will do really well with the Simply Music method. Frankly, I think that across the board, it doesn't really matter what the age, or the experience, or the background, or the gender of the person. If they are coachable, they are going to do well. If I had to look at my own students, would there be a subgroup that I consider to be my "best" students? I would say it would be those kids that came to me that had ADD, or ADHD. I'm not qualified to talk about it at a clinical level, but honestly, I interacted with these students as though they were no different from any student. In the Simply Music environment, I found no symptoms of any learning difficulties. Often, it seemed to be more the case that these students were really impacted by carrying around the psychology of believing that they were not capable at succeeding at things others were succeeding in. I don't have qualifications, nor empirical evidence, to support what I'm saying, but what I saw, again and again, were students who not only succeeded with Simply Music, but who were then impacted both psychologically and behaviorally by their success with this program. It became the norm for parents to say that, as their child succeeded, that they began to believe that they were capable of achieving other things. And that this translated into various other areas of their lives.

Also, homeschooling students seemed, as a subgroup, to do particularly well. I think that when parents fully embrace the responsibility of not only parenting their child but also formally educating their child, that they often are quite amenable to being coachable. That parent does particularly well in the three-way relationship I talked about earlier. When you marry a fully committed, coachable parent with a homeschool environment where there is intra-family learning taking place, the children are engaged and interactive in their responsibilities as part of the family. It becomes a sort of shared organism, and they bring that culture to piano lessons and their at-home practice. It seems to be a good mix.

B: Are adults coachable?

N: Coachablity and adulthood can be a complex path to navigate. As adults, all of us spend our lifetimes accumulating evidence of what we believe to be true about ourselves. Usually, being coachable requires that you be willing to step outside of those beliefs at times. The adult who is willing to do that is very exciting to teach. Adults who are coachable are not only great to teach, but they get so excited by the results that they become quite childlike. It's really cool; you get a dose of both an adult and a child in one. I love teaching adults, but mostly, I love coaching them.

I've trained a lot of adults and I usually ask the question, "Are you coachable?" For the most part, most adults believe they are coachable. I think, more accurately, adults are very good at what I call 'selective coaching'. In other words, regardless of what they say about coaching, how they actually *are* about coaching is something like, "I will completely follow your coaching provided that 1) I totally agree with it 2) I totally understand the reasons why and 3) it's convenient for me."

It's funny really, cause that is actually closer to the definition of "non-coachability". Being truly coachable often requires that you surrender to the coaching when you are not sure whether you agree or not. It requires you surrendering to the coaching when you absolutely do not understand why you are being asked to do any given thing. It also requires you to surrender to the coaching when it may well be completely inconvenient for you to do so. For me, working with adults that are truly coachable is one of the most exciting teaching experiences a person could have.

B: Does Simply Music place a lot of responsibility and accountability on the student?

N: Yes. I think that accountability and responsibility are often heard as having a quality of seriousness. Accountability and responsibility are often regarded as a strict discipline. Looking at it more deeply, I like the word "discipline", but I think we misunderstand it. If we look at the word discipline and its etymology, it connects with the idea of being a "disciple". The quality of a disciple includes the capacity to surrender – where surrender doesn't mean giving in or giving up, but, more so, making a powerful choice where one gives one's Self over to something. For a true disciple, it is real and natural to surrender. It is really the human identity that resists surrendering and that's where that whole concept of 'selective coaching' comes in. One of the things that happens in Simply Music is that we nurture the coaching relationship, not the 'selective coaching' relationship. In a well-managed environment, when a committed parent supports their child in powerfully surrendering to a committed coach, it produces extraordinary leaders. In this context, when you learn how to be a disciple of the program and surrender to the coaching, there is no better lesson for learning how to be a leader.

B: What does this look like in real life?

N: It manifests itself on various levels, all of which need to be developmentally appropriate. I'm not talking about needing to carry the weight of the world on your shoulders. I'm just talking about learning the simple mechanics of how to be coachable, as well as ensuring that the coaching is developmentally appropriate. In piano lessons, it can be as simple as requiring a child to practice for fifteen minutes each day at 4 pm. In other words, "I'm going to ask you to do certain things, you are going to agree to do those things. During the week you will surrender to what you agree to do and powerfully choose to do as you said." In Simply Music, one of our roles as both teachers and coaches is to successfully manage that outcome.

At the end of the day it reveals two things that are at the heart of Simply Music. They are 'the Method' – which provides the content of what you need to learn – and 'the Relationship' to the learning process. Coaching falls under the Relationship aspect of Simply Music. Quite simply, as a coach, I will make requests. Really, however, these requests are really requirements. You, as the coachable student, take on honoring those requirements and then, as a three-member team (teacher, student, parent), we will manage ensuring that it happens. There are tremendous life lessons that can be learned in this process and these lessons are learned intrinsically within Simply Music. We can be training students as young as five or six years of age and, with the simplest of projects, they can be learning extraordinary life skills.

B: If the parent doesn't do their job?

N: Well, there you go. That teaches the child an entirely different set of lessons.

B: Okay. So what is the most important thing to understand about Simply Music?

N: Well, with Simply Music it's never "one" thing – there are so, so many layers to this program. I think one of the things that is critical, at a deep level, is the perception of one's Self (whether we describe that as our humanness, or our spirituality, or our being). I assert that all human beings are musical beings. Regardless of your point of view, I think that it is fundamental to the design of human beings. Some would say that it is part of our Creator's design, if you will. This program is based on the premise that human beings are musical beings. In a traditional world, it is considered that some people are musical and some people aren't. By nature and by design, that creates a limit on the experience of one's humanness, and, I say, that this in itself has had profound cultural consequences. It has contributed to some of the illusions that impact us and that we are blind to. In contrast, coming from the premise that absolutely every single human being is deeply, naturally, and profoundly musical, that in itself to me is an empowering state – that I am a musical being. You know, if humanity could actually experience its musicality and merely regard itself as being a musical humanity, this alone would transform music education and self-expression on the planet.

B: What is the structure of this program?

N: The blueprint is really critical. It is not merely about music education. Imagine a circle divided up into four quadrants.

ARCHITECTURAL BLUEPRINT OF
THE SIMPLY MUSIC PROGRAM

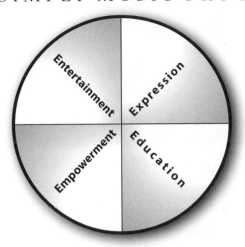

One of the quadrants, first and foremost is 'Expression'. This relates to the fundamental need to be musically self-expressed. The need to experience self-expression through music is universal, innate, and life-long. The opportunity here is to immediately access that level of expression, to nurture it, to foster it, to keep it alive, and to expand it. That is one critical component of the program.

The second quadrant is 'Entertainment' – entertainment for oneself and others. Music is a companion and the actual experience of playing music and hearing music is really an intimate experience for many people. For some people, the experience is a very deep form of prayer. Some people feel like they are talking to their Creator, talking to God. For others, it's contribution – when one can entertain themselves and entertain others. They experience it as a very deep sense of contribution. Simply Music gives a student this immediate experience and it is very empowering. It has profound benefits. Entertaining one's Self becomes a deeply personal and spiritual benefit. The idea of contributing to others through entertainment has profound implications.

The third quadrant of the circle is 'Empowerment'. When I say Empowerment, I am talking about self-responsibility. It's about being powerful and by that what I mean is being really effective in action, and function, in life. As a student, you learn how to navigate your way through long-term relationships, you develop the capacity and discipline of being able to pick yourself up and keep going. You learn to do that to the extent that you value what it is that you are pursuing. And as I said before, given that the need to be musically self-expressed is innate and life long, being musical is a unique companion. It's a companionship that one can have at both the human and spiritual level. One way we support that is in learning how to master long-term relationships.

The fourth quadrant would be the 'Education' experience. Obviously, there is a great deal of learning that occurs when one learns to play piano. Even though learning piano is an art, a craft and a science, more importantly, Simply Music is about 'learning a way of learning'. Our type of education, in a playing-based environment, is a natural way of learning. It's the way that we learn how to function in life, the way we learn on the field of action. We learn in the doing of things, not the theory of things. The Simply Music education experience is quite unique.

B: So if a parent brings their child to a Simply Music teacher for piano lessons, these things will develop?

N: It's organic to the program. That's how Simply Music's designed.

B: And your teachers do teach this way?

N: Yes, if they are willing to become who they need to become in order to teach Simply Music – it's how it's designed. It's quite extraordinary how committed our body of teachers actually is!

B: Simply Music emphasizes multiple genres of music.

N: We present a phenomenal variety of music. I think the future of music education, education as a whole, actually includes the need to become more inclusive. Some people say, "I know what I like." I think more accurately they are saying, "I like what I know." Often times, if we know little, we like little. Conversely, the more we are exposed to, the more we tend to expand what we like.

Learning how to understand and appreciate variety is a pretty important life lesson. Ray Charles once said something like, "all music has a soul, can you find the soul in everything?" In our program, we contribute to that journey by exposing students to the genres that are prevalent in our culture. As an overview, our students, from the very beginning, are exposed to classical, blues, jazz, contemporary, and gospel. They are also immersed in composition, improvisation, developing arrangements, as well as the vast world of contemporary accompaniment. I just want to make sure that the music we offer is broad-based enough so that we contribute to students having an appreciation for a diverse array of styles and genres and approaches to music.

I commonly ask students who have learned traditionally what kind of music they can play. Usually they can play classical pieces. I then ask them if they can play jazz. It's quite remarkable how often they say that their former teachers would not allow them to play anything other than the classical repertoire. I know of teachers who won't allow students to play jazz because that teacher doesn't consider it to be "real" music, or they consider anything other than classical music to be 'emotionally immature'. Wow, so much is lost in that perspective. I assert that it is critical to provide a broad and diverse selection of music to students. Our design, as human beings, is to learn in a very natural, broad-based manner. Simply Music gives us entrance into the diversity of music in a way that is congruent with our design. If you really look for it, you can start to see "sameness" in all music. A classical piece can be a blues piece that has its structure treated in a different way. A contemporary piece can be the same as a jazz piece, once again, treated in a different way. Learning to see the sameness in things allows us to expand as musicians and, in doing so, expand as people.

B: Why do you encourage Shared Lessons?

N: It's the most effective way of learning: to see life as a group. Can you imagine what it would be like if you were insulated from the group-aspect of life. Imagine if you went through a private lesson experience of life and then were turned out into the world as an adult. It's hard to imagine, really. You would have no understanding of how to relate to others, no experience at all in tolerating anyone else's point of view or perspective. No ability in how to conduct a relationship and understand the value of friendship, of support. No comprehension of the power of synergy and collective consciousness. All of these things come into play in the Shared Lesson environment. The ability to be immersed in different points of view, different learning processes, playing with others, learning from others, solving problems in a way that you wouldn't have thought – all of this occurs in a Shared Lesson environment. There is phenomenal peer support that's really important when one knows that one is part of a group that is moving forward at a particular pace. It supports students in being responsible for their own progress and for the role that it plays in the group as whole. So much more is learned. By nature, a more responsible learning emerges out of the group.

B: Some people may not be convinced about Shared Lessons. They might think they will go faster and learn more if they take private lessons.

N: The truth of the matter is that we've done private piano lessons for generation after generation. If private lessons, and this notion of 'individual attention', were the key to success, then we would have produced a culture where everybody would have learned to play. It is widely considered that piano has the highest failure rate of any taught subject we know.

All that's needed, to see the Shared Lesson concept in perspective, is to look at the results that it produces. The fact of the matter is that if you follow this program according to its design, you will produce unprecedented results. The typical, average, routine, ordinary result that Simply Music produces are students who, after twelve months of learning, have a repertoire of thirty to fifty songs covering all sorts of musical genres! These breakthrough results occur best in a Shared Lesson environment. The fact of the matter is what can be learned in the Shared Lesson environment, how it is learned, how the students are developed, as well as the dynamics and dimensions of the learning experience can never ever be achieved in the private lesson environment.

In Shared Lessons, you get the dimensions; you get the alternate points of view, the input, and the synergy of something being greater than the sum of its parts. It is similar to the value of being on the soccer team, basketball team, football team, and even in the homeschool environment. The intra-family, intra-team learning is pretty critical. The learned responsibility that can be nurtured in a Shared Lesson environment is unique. I know that I don't have to convince anybody. All I am interested in doing is stating what we've found to be true and consistent.

B: Do teachers like teaching Shared Lessons?

N: It's true that teaching Shared Lessons is distinctly different from teaching private lessons. For the teacher who is willing to expand themselves and discover who they need to be in order to successfully teach Shared Lessons, the results are abundant and absolutely worthwhile. Those who do this typically make comments like, "Now I understand how energizing this is for me, how much more efficient this is for me, how educationally better it is for the student, how far more broad-based the experience is, how more interactive it is, how more socializing it is, how much easier to teach and easier to learn it is," etc., etc. That is the shared, collective experience of the teachers that discover how to effectively teach Shared Lessons. This is not just an improvement to me; it's a geometric increase. Geometric leaps in the benefits. It's not even comparable to what private lessons achieve.

B: There is a lot of acceptance in the homeschool community. Why do you think this is so?

N: What we offer is important to a great many parents, who do or don't homeschool, but it's true that we see a concentrated acceptance of this within homeschooling families. I think it's because they function as a close-knit community and I think we achieve acceptance within this community because of the quality of education we offer. That is, it's a methodology that impacts the whole child. The learning experience offers extraordinary time efficiency. You get a very big 'return on your investment' with Simply Music. Just to start with, within a few lessons, you learn a handful of songs. The results are extraordinary and far-reaching and it's quickly very evident. This is a valid, credible curriculum that has both depth and breadth. I think this is a program that also nurtures children in a unique manner. It seems to be a widely shared value with homeschooling parents to encourage their children to grow up understanding the importance of service; making a contribution as a person, as one family, as many families, as society as a whole. Homeschooling families like the fact that Simply Music allows their children to share learning and share playing. Other families use it as an integral part of their spiritual commitment, such as using the method as a pathway to develop worship leaders. There are many things that homeschool families value and are looking for in a curriculum. It appears as though Simply Music is presented in a manner that is consistent with what they consider to be important.

B: Does Simply Music prepare students to be musicians of the future?
N: Absolutely.

B: How does the Simply Music student read music in comparison to a student who has learned traditionally?
N: Well, the first thing to know is that I never developed

252

Simply Music to be a breakthrough in sight-reading. I make very few claims about the efficacy of Simply Music and its approach to teaching students how to read. Having said that, it is very common for Simply Music teachers, who were already advanced readers of music, to say that they are better readers now as a result of going through our reading program. I think that our reading program, if it is taught properly, is appropriately challenging and yet, quite simple. Certainly it is very effective!

Our approach to reading involves two parts. We firstly teach rhythm; we then teach pitch using an intervallic system. We are not the only program that teaches music reading like this. There are some programs that teach rhythm first; there are other programs that teach pitch using an intervallic approach. To me, using intervals as a basis of learning how to read music is the way of the future. It seems to me that our existing acronymic and mnemonic approach is a dinosaur and has inherent design flaws that can never be resolved inside that system. Even so our entire program differs greatly from other programs. I would never say that teaching rhythm first or teaching an intervallic approach is unique, because it isn't. However, clearly what separates Simply Music from any other program from what I have seen is the fact that we teach students to read music using a generative approach.

B: How does Simply Music teach students to read? What is an interval?

N: In essence, we teach people how to read by teaching them how write. Reading is a receptive action; writing is a generative action. I assert that when we develop our generative ability, it exponentially expands our receptive ability. In essence, whatever happens inside the Simply Music reading program has a generative foundation at its base. At a practical level, our approach to teaching is quite simple. Firstly, let's take a look at reading rhythm. If you look at reading rhythm, for the most part, the vast majority of music uses mostly whole, half, quarter, eighth, and sixteenth notes. It's rare to ever see thirty-second, sixty-fourth, or one-hundred-and-twenty-eighth notes. Although we have to factor in ties, dotted notes, and rests, in reality we are only really dealing with five rhythmic elements – whole through sixteenth notes.

Now, let's talk about reading pitch, but let's look at the traditional approach first. Currently, traditional methods use the letters FACE as a means of learning the notes written in the spaces between the five lines of the treble clef. Unfortunately, the FACE acronym only works in the treble clef and no longer works in the bass clef. For the bass clef, we have to learn a new acronym. However, neither of these acronyms works in the ledger lines above the treble clef. Again, we have to create a new acronym. And of course, none of these acronyms work in the ledger lines below the treble clef, or the ledger lines above the bass clef, or the ledger lines below the bass clef. In other words, a new acronym would be needed for each of the six, distinct regions across the full piano score. I say that this is an inherent design flaw.

Now in contrast, with Simply Music's approach, we work with intervals in a particular manner. Let's firstly talk about intervals. An interval is a distance from one note to the next. It's a term that is a standard of measure in music (being able to quantify it, determining how far one note is from another). In a playing-based environment, we are building a framework of being able to recognize intervals readily. Given the architecture and design of the curriculum, as well as all of the compositions,

254

they play a critical role in the process. Students have already established a kinesthetic relationship to intervals without even knowing it. As such, when we introduce formal music reading, we are really just bringing a new language to an already developed skill. Instead of seeing music as shapes and patterns, we are now going to see the distances between notes as simple intervals.

The great thing about our approach to using an intervallic system is that the language we use has only five components to it, 'unison through fifths'. These five components, this one language, maps directly onto the fingers, it maps directly onto the keyboard, and without any alteration whatsoever, it maps onto each of the seven regions across the whole spectrum of written music. Ultimately, if you can develop a generative relationship to the five components of rhythm and the five-interval language of pitch and marry these with Simply Music's generative approach to writing/reading, then pretty well you have a handle on a fantastic foundation of learning how to read music.

B: And Simply Music waits one to two years to teach reading...?

N: We take as long as is needed to build a foundation of playing. For some students, we introduce reading at around the eighteen month mark; sometimes it could be few months earlier, sometimes a few months later. It's not at all about my agenda nor anybody else's agenda. It's all about introducing reading when it's developmentally appropriate for the student.

B: What if a parent wants their child to read music from the very beginning?

N: It's quite common for parents to ask about how soon it will be before their child begins to read. I say that even though that this is the prevailing thinking, it doesn't fully take into account the complexities and consequences of starting beginning students in a reading-based approach. Using music reading as a starting point has been the way 'it's been done' for many, many generations. It just doesn't make sense to me, and for the most part, it seems that the vast majority of people, of any age, who start in a reading-based program typically struggle with the experience. So many people who begin in a reading-based environment never really learn how to play. Too many lose their interest and desire to learn music forevermore. While it's common for many traditional music teachers to say that music is a language, in truth, many of them aren't really treating it as though it actually *is* a language. If we were to recognize and treat music as a language, we'd be using an approach similar to a way in which all of us learn how to speak.

You and I learned to talk and were speaking for years before we began learning to spell. In essence, Simply Music is doing the same thing. We say, "Let's build a foundation of self-expression through music. Let's build a direct, personal and intimate relationship with the instrument, let's develop and nurture our innate relationship to our musicality and have that manifest as a vast repertoire of great sounding music. With that as our basis, introducing the symbols of music reading makes a whole world of sense. The student is now bringing symbolic representation to what they already do and do well. Ultimately, the results speak for themselves. And if a parent insisted on their child learning to read music as a starting point, then, no problem, it would allow us to see, before we even start, that Simply Music isn't the right fit for what this parent is wanting for their child. And whether I agree with that or not, frankly, is

256

irrelevant. Parents have to do what they think is right and every parent is entitled to that.

B: What about an adult who doesn't believe they can learn how to read? They've tried to self-teach, take lessons, and still cannot read.

N: First, it's a normal thing for people to say that they've tried the reading thing and they "failed". Simply Music addresses this problem by having the student understand that we are going to be looking at music through an entirely different lens. We delay the reading process and immerse the adult student in a playing-based environment. In this environment, we give them tools to use. We help them see patterns and shapes on the keyboard. Without them even knowing it, we are training them to visualize intervals; we are training the intervallic approach into the hands, which then becomes the system we use in Simply Music to teach reading. If adults are willing to let go of the acronym/mnemonic approach from their past, follow the coaching, and build a playing-based foundation, and use that foundation inside of Simply Music's generative approach, then, they too will learn how to read music. Period!

B: What about teaching Simply Music? Why would someone want to teach Simply Music over traditional lessons?

N: Because it's uniquely and profoundly satisfying. There is an intrigue aspect to it, too. It is an intriguing thing to teach because it uses such a different set of tools than what has been used in the more traditional approaches. Very often a person who comes from a traditional background has had certain limitations with their experiences. Often times they have been confined to a classical music experience. What we are going to do is give them access and insight into contemporary, accompaniment, blues/jazz, improvisation, composition, gospel, ballads, arranging, etc. Often times, working with such a vast array of genres and styles is not something that they've had experience with. It's exciting for them.

The main thing, however, is that in the traditional realm, students and teachers would have to go through the 'endurance marathon' that is so common in the traditional, reading-based environment. In stark contrast, with Simply Music, teachers will have their students playing great-sounding music from their very first lessons. That is an extraordinarily empowering experience! It's an experience where you actually feel like you are making a difference. The students and parents know it because they communicate and acknowledge the impact that you are having on their lives.

B: What are the teachers like?

N: I see our teachers in four main categories. If I took a snapshot of any one hundred of our teachers, I would say fifty would be considered advanced musicians. Perhaps these fifty people would have music degrees in performance, theory, and/or pedagogy. They may have come out of recognized music teaching institutions and, for the most part, music has been their lives. That would be 50% of our teachers. The other 50%, I would break up into 25%, 20%, and 5%. 25% of them would be accomplished musicians. They studied on their own when they were younger, developed themselves and now have escalated up to a successful music position, i.e., a music director, a performer or recording artists, etc. The 20% would be considered socially competent players. They learned when they were young and continued playing, perhaps for the local church, parties, recitals, or school events. They kept music in their lives. Then, about 5% would be considered rudimentary or novice players, essentially new to the experience.

B: What level of expertise do teachers need to have before considering a Simply Music career?
N: Basic playing skills. So, even if a person has a limited repertoire, but it can be played in a musical manner – steady, smooth, and even – then that's enough of a musical foundation to begin the training process, provided that those songs have been learned with the playing-based approaches and domain.

B: How is it possible for a relatively inexperienced musician to be a successful teacher?
N: I'm fully aware of the fact that, given the existing paradigm of music education, it doesn't seem realistic for a less experienced musician to successfully teach others to play. Frankly, even considering how this could be possible can pose a new type of challenge for those whose background is based on traditional thinking and methods. However, as is the case when introducing any breakthrough methodology or technology, the idea of teaching Simply Music requires a willingness to consider things from an entirely different perspective.

Let's step back and look at an overall summary of how it works. We examine the very core of musicality and musicianship in a totally new light. We reinterpret music into a new 'playing-based' language. This in itself is a profound departure from the traditional 'reading-based' approach.

In addition to its unique methodology, Simply Music also explores new perspectives in dealing with the behavior that surrounds learning and playing music. Naturally, this translates directly to the lesson environment, where both students and parents are able to interact with the long-term relationship of music learning in a new and far more effective light. In essence, the very approach that is taken and the learning paths that are used, are based on new thinking and new perspectives. If you are clear about that fact, then, it makes sense that what it takes for teachers to achieve outstanding results with students is profoundly different to what has been required in the past with traditional methods.

Look, as I said earlier, many of our teachers are advanced musicians and many have had an extensive career in traditional teaching. But that's not necessarily what's needed in order to be a great Simply Music teacher. There are certain traits that are shared across the board by our most successful teachers. I find four things that are common and I am listing them in order of priority. First and foremost: a love of people. Second, that they value music and what it contributes to life. Third, that they are willing to think new things and see things from a new perspective. Fourth, that they are coachable. When those qualities are present, the result is that training to be a Simply Music teacher is an experience that has far-reaching impact. Many of our teachers commonly report that this program has made a significant and positive difference to areas of their lives that they never imagined would be affected.

B: How are teachers trained?
N: They are trained using a combination of things; audio materials, printed materials, audio-visual materials, phone coaching calls, etc. In conjunction, there is a library of resources of shared experiences of other colleagues – regular, open access, connectivity with the entire Simply Music teacher

community. Then the experience of teaching itself is training. There are workshops, symposia, conference calls, as well as email and forum boards that are added to and updated daily. Simply Music's training and support system is vast.

B: When training begins, what do you recommend on a weekly basis for the teacher?

N: The beginning teacher typically spends a portion of each day going through the training materials that are provided. These materials not only instruct on how to teach the program, but also explore how to manage the behavioral relationships that surround the teaching process. They explore the functional aspect of administrating and managing their studio. They also explore the promotional aspect of communicating to the public at large. There is daily content that they are immersed in, that is supported by weekly phone calls over the first month or so.

B: What about on an on-going basis?

On an on-going basis, teachers continue the on-going immersion in the modular content of the curriculum as a whole – the curriculum is vast! They also develop themselves by attending workshops, being on conference calls and chat sessions, attending events, etc. An extraordinary support is the one-on-one personal relationships they have with individual teachers from within the community. Simply Music provides an array of systems that allow teachers to connect with one another and build powerful, supportive and educational relationships. And, as desired, there is the momentary, hourly, daily, weekly access to Simply Music's system that engages the entire, worldwide, Simply Music teaching community in topical and relevant communication.

B: What is the relationship between the teacher/ parent/child like? How are Simply Music teachers trained to manage this relationship?

N: We train the teacher not to mandate or judge the choices of the parent. That's tremendously important. The best we can do is educate the student/parent. In this context I always regard the parent as a student, even though it may be the child who is having the lessons; it's always the parent who needs ongoing education in what Simply Music is and how to play their most powerful role in the process. It's really critical in Simply Music to understand the dynamics of relationships. You asked me a series of questions before about how Simply Music differs from traditional programs. One of the things that we talked about is that in the traditional environment, the learning is treated as one domain. I am saying that there are actually two distinct domains that have to be separated: one is the domain of 'The Method' and the other is the domain of 'The Relationship'. They must be understood separately. The idiosyncrasies of each need to be clearly distinguished and they must be managed independently from one another, simultaneously. What is needed to manage one, is different than the other. The parent has to be educated to understand that.

This isn't about just the method. There is nothing about the method that is going to inspire your child to want to practice everyday, month after month, year after year, and be so inspired to practice regardless of their feelings and wants. That's not going to happen. That's not how any long-term relationship works, whether you are a child or an adult. There's something else, something critical that needs to be introduced and kept alive. It's one of the things we do well.

B: So why do we need to understand these long-term relationships?

N: Earlier I talked about what parents need to understand. I know I'm repeating myself, but it's of extraordinary importance. Every long-term relationship is going to have to go through its ups and downs. These ups and downs are an absolutely essential experience in any and every successful, long-term relationship. In our current paradigm, people often relate to plateaus or valleys in the relationship as though they shouldn't happen or that something is "wrong" within the relationship. We have to educate the parent that these plateaus and valleys are of critical importance in learning how to navigate one's way through any and every long-term relationship. And regardless of whether the relationship is in a phase of a peak, a plateau, or a valley, all of these are equally normal, they're all natural, they're all necessary, and they're all temporary! Parents need to understand that they have an opportunity to play an extraordinary role in teaching their child lessons that will serve them well in any and all long-term relationships that they have for the rest of their lives. If a parent is not willing to play an active engaged role in their child's learning of long-term relationships, then that is none of my business. The best that I can do, however, is to let the parent know that their not being involved will play a role in the temporal nature of the experience. That is a lesson that will be learned and carried on into the next long-term relationship.

The challenge for the teacher is the ability to tell the truth. For a lot of people, they don't want to tell the truth because they feel uncomfortable. They want to stay comfortable and avoid the experience in the discomfort of being direct. They forfeit the opportunity to contribute to the parent and this in turn shapes the child's relationship to music and every other long-term relationship in their lives. It's amazing how much we sacrifice for comfort. It is my commitment to have the conversation about long-term relationships often enough, and long enough, so it sort of permeates the culture of the teacher body. Whilst teaching Simply Music includes unfolding the method, it is so very much about the nature of relationship and about communicating responsibility.

B: So teachers learn a lot about relationships…?

N: Yes they do, largely because there is an enormous component of this program that operates outside of 'The Method'. I call the Method the 'steps of the program'. Look at the circles: Method and Relationship. Relationship is possibly the most significant component of the Simply Music teaching experience because of the constant interaction and management of relationships. Simply Music explores how to manage the teacher/student/ parent relationship, including the simple dynamics and idiosyncrasies of long-term relationships. Simply Music manages the 'behavioral dimension', the way we are in relationships, who we are being in relationships. In the Teacher Training, we explore different types of communication that produce different outcomes. We explore what it means to tell the truth in a loving compassionate manner, instead of stating something real, but said in a way that is punitive. We look at the ways we hand over control, or 'territory', in ways that are detrimental to a successful

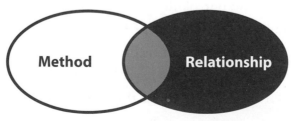

coaching relationship. We look at all of the many ways, and most subtle ways, in which teachers actually hand over the authority in the teaching environment to the student. Without even knowing it, teachers so often hand over the role of the coach, to the absolute most inappropriate person – the student.

B: Most Simply Music teachers are self-employed. Do teachers have to want to be self-employed?

N: Sometimes people need to learn how to see the remarkable benefits that are available when you are self-employed and what it is that you create with that. I heard a statistic stating that 97% of the entire work force is employed by 3% of the people. There is a commitment and power to being self-employed. People learn how to embrace, through responsibility, the opportunity of self-employment. It is a unique journey when you are responsible for yourself. There is an entirely different set of choices that become available when one is self-employed as a Simply Music teacher. An education occurs that's unique. You learn how to market/promote your business, manage your business, manage people, manage relationships, and navigate your way through a myriad of a curricula that has so many layers. There are a lot of life skills and practical skills. You also develop your own musicianship in the process. It's pretty cool.

B: What makes the Simply Music opportunity unique?

N: The way I set it up. I decided that licensing would give us the ability to control the framework for the intellectual property and give a great deal of freedom of self-employment to the teacher. We only control the content of the Intellectual Property. Teachers have the freedom and independence to choose when they work, where they work, how little or how much they charge, how few or how many students they have, etc. It's up to them. I like that teachers have that level of ownership.

B: Is teaching Simply Music different from teaching at the advanced, concert-level?

N: Yes, very. And Simply Music is not going to be all things, for all people, at all times. I think that this is a really important thing to know. However, it's not necessarily a good idea to have a Ph.D. in math teaching elementary math at Kindergarten. If someone's expertise is at a concert level, they are probably best at contributing to students who are interested in, and ready for, the body of distinctions that that teacher is capable of imparting. So for the concert-level teacher, who is in their element at that level, it may not be the best fit for them to teach Simply Music. It might be undercapitalizing what they have to contribute in the area of their expertise.

I know that for the concert-level player, maintaining their level of performance requires a vocational commitment. These are people who might spend six to twelve hours a day, every day, developing the highest level of excellence in the most complex and subtle distinctions of music expression, articulation, and performance. These are the Olympic athletes, the Vikings, the extraordinary performing artists. I am in awe of what it takes at that level. I have experienced performances of concert-level pianists and it boggles my mind as to how accomplished they are.

But this level of performance is not the arena in which I am working. The vast majority of students are not interested in concert-level playing. And given that Simply Music is about the broader culture at large, I am focused on that which most of the planet is most interested in. And the vast, vast majority are very interested in the companionship of recreational music making.

266

The educational system that we have inherited was designed to produce adult, concert-level performance. Over time, many of the educational tenets of this approach have filtered down to become the social standard bearer for the community at large. As a result, there are standards and measures that might be appropriate for the budding concert pianist, however, these standards and measures are entirely inappropriate for most others. To tell the truth, I think that the current, prevailing platform is extraordinarily inappropriate for the vast majority of people.

And, frankly, when I have the opportunity to work closely with traditional teachers and they get to a point where they feel safe enough to reveal themselves, it is really common for these teachers to say that there is very little joy in what they do, very little freedom in their teaching, very little freedom and creativity in their own playing, and very little freedom and creativity in their students' playing. The majority of these teachers, when they get to the bottom line, see the need for transforming our cultural approach to music education.

B: What does a traditionally-trained teacher need to know about teaching Simply Music?
N: This is about a new paradigm in music education. It requires that the teacher be willing to look at the broader picture in an entirely new way. This program can be accessed by a vast majority of people. It immediately gives those people an entry-point into the broad arena of comprehensive musicianship; playing all sorts of musical styles, being able to read, write, transcribe, to understand scale and key signature, to work with lead sheets, etc. These people can play contemporary, classical, blues and gospel, and they can

compose and improvise and arrange, etc. We are going to achieve this by utilizing a new approach, new perspectives, and a new framework of thinking. If a traditionally trained teacher looks at Simply Music and tries to fit our program into what they already know, then they are going to have trouble. If they try to make this program conform to the prevailing array of inherited standards and measures, then they are going to have trouble. Clearly, this program requires everybody to look at music through a new lens, to be willing to just set aside what it is that they think they know. If a teacher is willing to do this, they have an opportunity to revolutionize their personal relationship to music, and to teaching, and transform the lives of other people in entirely new ways.

B: Do you see a difference between the community of traditional teachers as compared to Simply Music teachers?

N: Yes I do. We are a united community. That, in itself, is a big difference. I am not aware of any other piano teaching organization where there is an international and growing community of teachers, who teach under the umbrella of a common name, a common identity, the same curriculum, and an aligned vision that is focused on altering the culture of music education. Ours is a community of teachers who are immersed in the collaborative learning/teaching/sharing experience of Simply Music and its vision.

B: Anything else you want to say about your teacher body?

N: They are an amazingly committed group of people. They are committed to belonging to something that is 'up to something'.

They are committed to something that is up to fulfilling something. They are committed to bringing possibilities into reality, realizing a vision, being a cause of a new era. These are people who are committed to make a lasting difference. They are who make Simply Music what it is.

B: So then, how does Simply Music's vision fit into our current and future culture?
N: Well look, this is a vast conversation in and of itself. I'm pretty sure that I'm not going to "answer" the question, but here's one response. What I am looking to do with this program is open the doors to the masses in a way that has never been done before. And I think we can. It's said that 'a rising tide floats all boats'. And we are on the cusp of creating a rising tide in the form of a musical revolution. It's the possibility of a world where everybody routinely acquires musical self-expression and retains it as a lifelong companion. It's the opportunity to create a breakthrough in the global relationship to the role that music plays in our lives. It's the possibility of causing a new era of engagement, creativity, self-expression, and fulfillment. And then, at a practical level, it's the opportunity to create cultures of people who consistently expand their musicianship. For some, it will include elevating to the highest levels of performance. It will include, at an organic level, creating more composers, songwriters, more performing artists, more social players, more people learning and studying music. The role of expanded musical self-expression will be prevalent at all levels and in all fields of education. Music education will be woven throughout our learning infrastructures. And over time, a new world will emerge. For example, I can see a time when expectant mothers will truly

understand the unique and critical role that music can play in prenatal communication with their child. Parents will sing, and dance, and play music, with the knowledge that they are already having a powerful impact on their unborn child's development. Children will routinely be born into homes where music is both played and learned. Self-expression through music will become the norm and its by-product will manifest as a new generation of creative and collaborative thinkers who will bring an entirely new perspective to solving the problems of our day. And, I say that there are a great many people who would love to play a role in creating that future.

§§§

On the following page is Simply Music's foundation statement for the organization that Neil Moore created.

SIMPLY MUSIC
FOUNDATION STATEMENT

Simply Music is the largest, playing-based music education institution in the world. Our foundational premise is that all human beings are deeply and naturally musical.

Our Future
♦ We are creating a breakthrough in the global relationship to music.
♦ We are creating a new era of engagement, creativity, self-expression and fulfillment.
♦ We are creating a world where everyone plays.

Our Organization
♦ We are a vision-driven pioneer and world-leader in music education and participation.
♦ We contribute to the quality of life of our employees, educators and associates.
♦ We treat people with dignity and respect, we provide opportunities for people to nurture their existing strengths, and we support people in moving beyond the challenges that thwart their ability to grow and develop.
♦ We are a living example of the highest levels of professionalism, integrity and graciousness in our dealings with people, and we set a precedent in the quality of service provided to all.

Our Guiding Principles
♦ Everything we do is done with a commitment to excellence.
♦ We recognize that being profitable is essential to fulfilling our vision.
♦ We build relationships with those who support our Guiding Principles.
♦ We build local and worldwide relationships that transform our communities.